A Surrendered Life

Finding Freedom, Hope and Purpose
After Abortion

By

Patricia K Layton

A Surrendered Life
Published by Pat Layton
Copyright 2020 by Pat Layton, Third Edition
This title is also available as an eBook for Kindle.
Visit www.patlayon.net

Requests for information should be addressed to
pat@patlayon.net

Trade Paperback ISBN 978-0-9982342-5-0
eBook ISBN

Library of Congress Cataloging-in-Publication Data

Printed in the United States of America
2014 Baker Books—Revised 2020

Endorsements for A Surrendered Life and Surrendering the Secret: Healing the Heartbreak of Abortion

Surrendering the Secret breaks open the secret that so many women and men suffer with. It is a secret that we allow Satan to control...and he will continue to control it until we truly surrender that secret to Christ and allow Him to use our past for His glory. Our stories need to be told. I believe this book will inspire the confidence we need to share those stories and find healing in the power of Christ."
Abby Johnson Founder, And Then There Were None and Author, Unplanned

"*Surrendering the Secret* is a must read, providing insight into the journey of healing the wounds of a post-abortive woman. She is captivating the hearts of many men and women through her own transparency, testimony and life experiences. Her love is felt with every turn of the page."
Shari Rigby
Author *Consider the Lilies*
Actress, October Baby, Overcomer and National Speaker

I have loved Pat Layton's heart from the first day I met her many years ago. Praying God will use *Surrendering the Secret* and *A Surrendered Life* to reach every woman who is in pain from a past decision. I believe in this message and contagious passion that keeps Pat awake at night to help those who are hurting.
Faith Whatley, LifeWay Christian Resources

A Surrendered Life is a key to unlocking the secret places of millions of women's hearts hurting from abortion. The waters of healing tears need to overflow these secret places, unlocking an army of women ready to Do Justice and Be a Witness. Healing comes from confession and surrender."
Allan E. Parker President
The Justice Foundation

Pat Layton has spent a lifetime on the frontlines helping women find help, hope, and a truth that "sets you free. *A Surrendered Life* will help women discover that the surrendered life is the path to their future happiness and wholeness as an individual, in their marriage and family.
Pam Farrel
International speaker, author of over thirty books

A Surrendered Life is a must read for anyone who has endured an abortion and all those who love someone who has. Filled with personal transparency and biblical truth, these pages take the reader on a journey toward freedom where there is hope for real healing. God bless you as you read and oh, how I pray for the sweet lives this book will reach.
Angela Thomas
Best-selling Author and Speaker

Pat is an incredible woman with an incredible passion for helping women who hurt. She has surrendered her life to free women from the bondage of their emotional pain. It is our hope that *A Surrendered Life* will give thousands of women renewed hope and a bright future."

Mark Merrill and Susan Merrill
Author of All Pro Dad , iMom and Family First

If I could hand pick the perfect person to write a book about healing after an abortion, it would be my friend, Pat Layton. Her advice is tender, realistic, and filled with hope. As a woman who has experienced the depths of emotions an abortion brings, I am so thankful for the *Surrendering the Secret* Bible study and for Pat's new book *A Surrendered Life.*
Lysa TerKeurst-
NY Times Bestselling author and President of Proverbs 31 Ministries

I have personally heard many stories from people whose lives have been transformed by *Surrendering the Secret.* You will be blessed too by A Surrendered Life. Having known Pat Layton for years, her compassion, wisdom and inspirational testimony will fill you with hope. A Surrendered Life will help you find freedom from the heartache of abortion.
Craig Altman, Senior Pastor Grace Family Church
Tampa, FL

A Surrendered Life will lead you on a journey of freedom and hope. Although the topic of abortion can be politically charged, divisive and often avoided in the church, for the millions of women and men who have experienced it, it is a walk of shame that needs to be redeemed by God's grace. In her book, *A Surrendered Life*, Pay Layton shares her story, a transparent 8-step process that leads those who have endured the heartbreak of abortion and those who care, to a place of redemption and hope. Whether you part of the estimated 43% of women who are hiding the secret of a past abortion, or not, chances are high that abortion has touched the life of someone you love. Buy a copy today and discover practical steps and biblical truths that will ushers thousands into a place of healing.
Renee Swope
Author, Speaker & Radio Co-host Proverbs 31 Ministries

As a filmmaker, your job is to use the craft of storytelling to expose an issue that needs to be looked at and talked about, but after people are talking, they need the right people to talk to. So many people who watch October Baby desperately need that and that's why I'm grateful for Pat Layton. Her work with those individuals who have experienced the pain from abortion is unparalleled. And the healing I see coming out of her ministry to so many post abortive people reassures me that those who need to talk are in very good hands.

Andrew Erwin, Filmmaker

In my counseling and coaching I have become all too familiar with pain and loss caused by issues from the past. Statistics reveal that for millions of men and women destructive anxiety, fear, guilt, and shame are the result of a past abortion. In *A Surrendered Life* Pat Layton offers real hope and healing for those who've faced abortion and for those who love them. Drawing from her personal experience Pat provides eight proven steps that enable those who struggle to move from the loss and pain to healing and freedom

Georgia Shaffer
Author, Speaker, PA Licensed Psychologist, Certified Life Coach

DEDICATION

This book is dedicated to my Jesus. The ONE who Set Me Free and to the "Surrendered Life" of our firstborn daughter. Because of His Grace, I will hold you.

"Oh my goodness Lord. Your majesty overwhelms me. Your mercy literally allows my life to go on. Your grace covers my utter failure. Your blessings astound me. Your call on my life brings my knees to the ground. Your glory draws my arms to the sky. Your anointing makes me dance. Your vision takes me to repentance. Your death gives me life and your life gives me purpose. Most of all my Lord, your love gives me all that I need. Your word gives me direction. Your blessing gives me freedom. Your reflection challenges my pursuit of holiness. Your supernatural power gives me rest"

I surrender my life to you.

Pat

This book IS for everyone!
If You Have Not had an Abortion - SOMEONE in your world has.

With statistics being what they are, an estimated 40% of women of childbearing age have had at least one abortion. These are your sisters, daughters, friends and even mothers. They all have men involved.

By reading this book you will:
- Understand why women and men make a choice for abortion.
- Learn how post abortion heartbreak may be showing up in your life or the lives of your loved ones.
- Understand the eight steps to healing from a past abortion.
- Be equipped with the tools to guide a discussion about the heartbreak of abortion.
- Learn ways to make a difference in your home, church or community in this heartbreaking holocaust of life.

Regardless of your personal experience with abortion, the eight-step method of healing and restoration used in Surrendering the Secret will certainly apply at some level in your own life. You may not have had an abortion but chances are even greater than 43% that you have had some life changing loss or heartbreak. The steps used in *A Surrendered Life* and *Surrendering the Secret* will minister to you and take your walk of faith to a new level.

Contents

1

A Surrendered Life

It was a fabulous Florida day. Springtime. My windows were rolled down and my Christian music was blaring. I was singing and praising God out of a new heart filled with hope and thanksgiving. I had just surrendered my life to Christ just a few months ago and within six months of my rebirth; my husband and two sons had also turned to Christ. Our lives had dramatically changed as a result and it seemed that God was suddenly pouring out His blessings on our home and family. Things seemed to finally be taking a turn for the better after a long season of looming dead ends and pending divorce.

Little did I know that secrets of our past, long stuffed away, were about to all come crashing in and put my family at risk all over again.

My new Christian journey seemed to be affecting every part of my life, just one of which was the radio station that broke into the air from my car speakers. I had moved from rock to praise music and was very intrigued by the style of chatter between the radio moderators. They prayed. They quoted Bible verses. They teased about bad habits. I had jumped out of my car for a few minutes to run an errand. When I slid back into the driver's seat, my praise music had changed over to a talk show. It was a conversation that would change my life forever. I was shocked to hear three women talking with a moderator, sharing their stories about past abortions.

I could barely breathe as I listened. My heart raced. What in the world was this? Abortion! Why were they talking about abortion on a Christian radio station?

What does God have to do with abortion?

What does abortion have to do with God?

What had happened to my praise music?

Little did I know as I pulled my car to the side of the road to listen that my life would never be the same.

A few months later, after I'd successfully stuffed my emotions down again, I strolled into the Christian bookstore with one thing in mind: to find a book that would help me fix my husband! He really needed fixing. We had been Christians for at least a year and I just knew God still wanted to do a lot of work on HIM! As I stepped into the bookstore that morning, I ran smack into a display of books all focused on one topic- you guessed it- abortion. Here it was again- abortion, a topic I had managed to avoid for over seven years.

The book standing front and center of this bookstore display was titled "*Will I Cry Tomorrow?* Healing Post Abortion

Trauma. Oh my gosh. Here it was again. That word-abortion. In a Christian bookstore. How could that be? I had managed to go for seven years and never saw that word, much less said it. At the time, I had no idea WHY, but I grabbed it up, dashed to the register, paid the bill, and raced for the door.

Over the next five or six hours, I devoured that book from cover to cover. Although I can remember it like it was yesterday, it is close to impossible for me to describe the feelings that stirred in my heart and mind over that day of reading. Shock, unbelief, fear, disgust and certainly nausea are just a few that come to mind. After finishing, I fumbled my way to the bathtub and filled it halfway with very hot water. The rest of the tub I filled with my own hot tears as I sobbed for hours. I wept for my aborted child. I wept for my loss. I wept for the lies. I wept for the author of the book I'd read. I wept for the abortionists involved in our lives. I wept for the world. I wept for the pain of my Savior, my Lord, and my Redeemer, Jesus Christ.

When I had cried all that I could cry, I handed my heart to God.

You may be someone who can identify with those hours in my life. That process in time that I allowed God to shine His light into the darkest places of my past. I allowed Him, like He describes in Psalms 139 to "make even my darkness light to Him".

Maybe you are someone like me who experienced the devastation of a past abortion; maybe abortion is not your secret and not in your personal past. Maybe you have abuse or abandonment in your past. Maybe it is childhood brokenness in your family. Rape. Substance abuse.

3

Immorality, adultery or divorce. Or maybe, you are someone who just LOVES someone who has had a past abortion. Maybe you are the Grandparent of an aborted child or the brother, sister, friend or neighbor. In my travels with speaking and writing, I have discovered that the process used for post abortion recovery is the process God uses without fail, to set us free from any past heartbreak or loss. So, if you have NOT personally experienced an abortion, get ready to have God do a work in your own life as you increase your knowledge for someone else. One thing I know is that it's impossible for you NOT to know someone who has experienced the horror and heartbreak of a past abortion. After forty Years of legalized abortion in America, estimates tell us that one in three women have had an abortion. Over 50 million lives have been destroyed. For every single abortion there is a mother and a father; grandmothers and grandfathers; brothers, sisters and friends.

Wherever you fall in that description, I pray that you will walk with me. Walk with me on a journey of understanding the truth about abortion and how it's roots can be found in the Bible way back to the book of Genesis. Most of all walk with me on a journey through healing and restoration. A journey of hope and a journey towards life.

It matters that you do. It matters to those who need to hear the truth. It matters to those who didn't hear it in time and to those whose lives will be rescued because they do.

Let's get started by going backwards.

Keeping the Past Where It Belongs?

Strolling down memory lane can be wonderful. Memories come and go when we least expect them. The smell of warm baked bread takes us back to grandma's house and we're eight years old again. Attending a hometown high school reunion inspires us to drive up and down streets pointing out our elementary school, a dear friend's home, or our favorite burger hangout to a bored spouse or friend.

In the same way, bad memories—despite our efforts to suppress them—ebb and flow in our minds and hearts, bringing pain instead of happiness. Among all the memories we could name, abortion stands alone.

My most haunting memory concerns an abortion I had when I was twenty-three years old. I remember the smell of the room, the looks on the faces of women sitting around a dark reception room, the sounds of soft lonely tears and the coldness of the building. Oddly enough, I still remember the dirty tennis shoes worn by the "nurse" who shoved a clipboard intake questionnaire coldly in my direction, and my petrified flight out the door in search of a "nicer abortion." Unlike the sweet memories of elementary school, those darker memories have been seared deeply in my heart and soul for many years.

Tragically, traumatic memories have more than a passing impact on our lives. Research confirms my own experience. Abortion memories continue to not only haunt but also substantively damage women and men for years and decades.

After years of trying everything else to put the past behind me, I learned that to experience healing I had to go back and face my past. Only then did I become free to move into the future. The thought of going back to deal with emotions I had worked so hard to bury frightened me and seemed overwhelming. What good could come from that? Why would anyone go back?

The Bible contains a story about a woman named Hagar. Her story does not involve abortion, but it does contain many of the emotions engendered by it. Hagar was a woman much like me and maybe like you. The first parallel with abortion occurs when her dream for family and motherhood did not go the way she planned—the way she had dreamed since she was a little girl.

A woman named Sarai owned Hagar, an Egyptian slave. Sarai could not have a child, so she persuaded her husband Abram to father a child through the slave girl. After Hagar became pregnant, she began to feel and act superior to her owner. "Then Sarai said to Abram, 'you are responsible for my suffering! I put my slave in your arms, and ever since she saw that she was pregnant, she has looked down on me. May the LORD judge between me and you.' ⁶Abram replied to Sarai, 'Here, your slave is in your hands; do whatever you want with her.' Then Sarai mistreated her so much that she ran away from her" (Genesis 16:5-6, HCSB).

We see the second parallel to abortion when Hagar responded to what she saw as a hopeless situation by running away as hard and fast as she could. I don't think she stopped to consider where she might end up or what consequences her choice would bring. She just responded to her pain and loss in desperation and panic. I can identify because I too have been like Hagar.

Perhaps you too, like thousands of women every day, have responded to panic with the choice to have an abortion. It may have been a choice that seemed to be your only hope, your only option, but desperation doesn't make for sound choices. Just like Hagar, many of us felt lost, alone and betrayed. We ran, and with little direction, made a choice that would change us forever.

We choose abortion for many reasons: as a response to shame about our behavior and lifestyle patterns, as an act of rebellion or control, or because a husband, boyfriend or parents have given us an ultimatum. We choose abortion to protect someone else or we choose abortion as an act of confused freedom. Many of us have been told abortion is a simple solution to the problem of an unwanted or unexpected pregnancy, the easy out, the quick fix.

Eventually we find out the truth. Abortion leads us to the same place Hagar's choice to run led her, to the middle of nowhere.

My Story

My story wasn't so different. I chose abortion just after my 23rd birthday. I had lived a life of bad choices and immorality since I was fifteen. I grew up in an average home with a mother and a father who were married as young twenty something's in rural Savannah, Georgia. My parents stayed married for over fifty years until my Dad died nearly ten years ago. They were middle class, blue collar, God fearing folks. I have three younger sisters and lots of memories both good and bad.

My parents also came from fairly average American families—neatly woven on the outside but fairly messed up underneath. Their family backgrounds included alcoholism, tobacco and drug addiction, pornography, divorce, adultery and teen pregnancy in the legacy that affected their childhood and mine.

I've learned that family "junk" goes back to Adam and Eve and is truly God's specialty. He uses our personal junk to bring us to good and healed places. My teenage immorality led to a teenage marriage, teenage motherhood, eventual abandonment, and finally to becoming a single teenage mother of one simply precious son.

As I cared for my son and with the help of my parents returned to school and college, I met the next "Man of My Dreams." The two of us continued in the lifestyle that we had both grown accustomed to in the 70's and soon found ourselves in an unplanned pregnancy. The good news was that we were in love and engaged to be married when we found ourselves pregnant. The bad news was that even though I was "in love" and had agreed to be married, I was not "in trust". I had already been left all alone holding a swaddling babe wrapped in a blanket. I was not about to go that route again.

I had fought diligently for "a woman's right to choose" abortion while in college. During those days I could wax eloquent about why women should have a right to determine when and if, they wanted to have a child. I proclaimed we ultimately should control "our own bodies." I was so convincing that my opinions had even been published as a Pro-Choice advocate in a local woman's newspaper.

When I discovered I was pregnant just prior to my wedding day I made what I thought was a logical and healthy decision, to abort. As far as I was concerned, my future husband had no vote. He silently obliged, a choice we would both live to regret.

I told you earlier about my first visit to a newly opened neighborhood abortion clinic that I deemed dirty and dark. That abortion facility left such a nasty taste in my mouth I decided to approach my own OB/GYN, the one who had delivered my firstborn son, to obtain the "safe and legal" abortion that I had fought so hard to legalize.

Just like my future husband, my OB/GYN never questioned my decision. He simply set the date for two weeks after my wedding day. A marriage certificate meant little to me in terms of a man staying for the long haul, so I accepted the date. My husband and I went on our honeymoon pregnant with a date for an abortion on our calendars when we returned. It was not the honeymoon of every little girl's dreams. The marriage would not be either, not for a very long time.

We planned to drop our son off at Kindergarten and arrive at the hospital at 7am. My husband had begun the steps to adopt my son before we ever married. I paid the extra money to be put to sleep during the abortion procedure. Even with that, we were told that "the procedure" would only take "a few minutes." We planned pick our son up at school, go get some lunch and move on with life.

It would be our secret.

Instead, I woke up unable to move my body or speak. I had a tube stuck down my throat and a machine breathing for me. While my husband and my parents stood at the foot of my hospital bed the Dr explained that I had an allergic reaction to the anesthesia used to put me to sleep during the procedure. My breathing had stopped during surgery. I had to be admitted to the hospital. My new husband was forced to call my parents to pick my son up from school.

I still remember today the look on the faces of my mom and dad as they stood at the foot of my hospital bed. Shock. Shame. Fear. Loss. My secret was a secret no longer.

My feelings of embarrassment, shame, and even anger followed me out of that hospital. They did not leave for 7 long years.

My parents never said the word "abortion." I never said the word. My husband never said the word.

What happened next would close the casket of my heart and change my life forever.

If you've experienced abortion you know the term *casket of your heart* is more than a just mental picture. Depending on how long ago you had an abortion or multiple abortions, you have probably kept your secret buried deep inside your heart. Even if someone knows you most likely have never talked about it out loud. You have never wrestled verbally with the who, what, when, where or why of your choice to abort.

In this book I want to allow you the opportunity, or maybe the challenge, of digging into your abortion memory for the purpose of discovering some new things about God. Hagar learned in her situation. She trusted God and braved a return to her past. In the process Hagar discovered a new identity for God and relationship to God.

I didn't know that choosing abortion wasn't solving my problem. I was rather creating a whole new set of difficulties. Once we begin down the road of abortion, we have to run again, and again. Like a modern-day Hagar we run into the wilderness of fear, shame, abandonment, anger, and self-destruction. In a desolate lonely land, we become numb captives to our secret.

Hagar's flight to the desert left her at a spring beside the road. The angel of the Lord met her there and told her to return to Sarai and to submit to her authority. "The angel also said, 'You are now pregnant and will give birth to a son. You are to name him Ishmael (which means 'God hears'), for the LORD has heard your cry of distress...' Thereafter, Hagar used another name to refer to the LORD, who had spoken to her. She said, 'You are the God who sees me.' ... So Hagar gave Abram a son, and Abram named him Ishmael" (Genesis 16:11-15, NLT).

A Word to Male Readers

If you are a man reading this book, let us salute you. If you are a partner in an abortion, your participation may have ranged from actively pressuring her to abort to being helplessly opposed and excluded. Or you may be in a relationship with a woman who struggles with the results of a past abortion. Please don't feel picked on when I mention the male involvement. I will be talking more specifically about your role and your heart in an abortion decision in chapter nine but for now let me just get you to think on the story of Hagar from a man's perspective.

In the story of Hagar, we see something typical of many men's involvement in abortion. Abraham's main mark in the story was extreme passivity. When Sarai hatched the initial scheme, he simply went along. When Sarai regretted the situation his response to was "'Here, your slave is in your hands; do whatever you want with her'" (Genesis 16:6).

In dealing with post-abortion recovery, you may face difficult days. Your wife may go through great pain, and she may react negatively to you. You may be called upon for superhuman patience and love. What you absolutely must not do is become passive as Abraham did. Actively love, don't passively withdraw. The relationship you desire will be your reward.

A few other ways abortion affects men:

Abortion Steals and Destroys the life, the lineage of a man's legacy and name.

Abortion violates the core need of a man to provide and protect his wife and children.

Abortion separates the hearts of a man from the heart of the Father God by destroying trust, violating values and building barriers.

Lessons from the Wilderness

As we compare the experience of Hagar to the wilderness we wander today, abortion does not lead to a literal desert. It creates a wilderness we carry in our hearts and minds. When we carry a heavy burden, we naturally feel trapped by the shadows that surround us. Like Hagar, we grow weary, and feel ready to give up in despair and shame. As if that weren't enough, both Hagar's story and ours has a villain who always follows us into the wilderness. Instead of seeing the

"God who sees me" and the only One who never lets us go, we hear the inner voices of condemnation and shame ... and the lying voice of the tempter.

The amazing news is that God longs to come and rescue us. When God found Hagar abandoned and hopeless in the wilderness, He showed her that she must confront her pain, and stop trying to mask it. For every woman the mask looks a little different. God wants us to remove our masks, the pain we hide behind, and be FREE. He sets us free to love, free to heal, free to forgive and free to live.

Some women feel the sting of their choice for abortion every day. Others have completely disconnected from it. No matter how silent your pain, God's hears the cry of your heart. He sees you in your desert and feels your pain. God longs for you to look back on that difficult time in your life, and with Hagar to ask, "Have I truly seen the One who sees me?"

If you are a fellow traveler on the journey of recovery from abortion, I hope you will allow God to use this book and me in your life. Through the next few pages I will seek to be your guide, your angel in the desert, safely walking with you back to face the secrets, shadows, and shame that have kept you from the life God intended for you. Just like Hagar, you have a promise that God will personally meet you in your place of need.

The Bottom Line: Trusting the God Who Sees Me

If going back to find peace is so easy, why do we resist? We continue to hesitate for many reasons. We doubt God's heart toward us. After all the pain and struggles in our lives we ask ourselves, *if God is good, how could He have let this happen to me?* Given the way most of us were raised, we also focus on God's judgment with little understanding of His incredible desire and passion for us.

God longs to love you, and your love is safe with Him. His love is like nothing we have ever experienced. His love is unconditional and eternal. You can rest in God's arms, take comfort in His unfailing love, and hold His hand on your journey toward freedom.

Right now, make the choice for freedom. Summon the courage and make a new choice, a choice for your freedom. Chose the path of healing and peace, don't allow your life and dreams to die with a past mistake.

Remember you are not alone. Think of reading this book as a challenging mountain trek. Now is the time to confront our fear and pain and begin the slow, steady journey to the summit. It takes faith and courage to tackle this mountain. We're going to do this because the view from the top is worth the surrender.

This book will help you to get to the summit where the stigma of abortion is gone. In the process you will find personal healing or healing for someone you love. Together we can enjoy reconciliation with God and with our unborn children. In the process we find a life of secrets, shame, and shadows completely redeemed.

In chapter two, we'll take the first step by looking honestly at the trauma of abortion and how it may be affecting your life. We'll dig into some facts about physical, social, emotional, and spiritual aspects of abortion.

Every man and woman, who has chosen abortion as a way of escape, has been sold a lie. Lies create secrecy, bondage, darkness, and shame. God wants to set you free, but you will have to pursue your freedom through a sometimes-uncomfortable journey. You will not be alone. You have an entire team behind the pages of this book. Take a look at the Surrendering the Secret website www.surrenderingthesecret.com or join us on Facebook and let us know that you have begun this journey.

In Luke 1:79 the Scripture says that the plan of God is "To shine upon and give light to those who sit in darkness and in the shadow of death, to direct and guide our feet in a straight line into the ways of peace". God wants to direct your feet into that same light and peace, complete peace. A peace that doesn't allow anything to shame you or make you feel like you have felt as a result of past heartbreaks.

The plan of God is "to shine upon and give light to those who sit in darkness and in the shadow of death, to direct and guide our feet in a straight line into the ways of peace." Luke 1:79

He wants you to be free from all insecurity and fear. Through the pages of this book you and I are going to take a journey together, through a process that has set people FREE for over twenty years.

We are about to step out together to stand up and shout out to the world, "I AM FREE, I am healed, and I am whole. My God has seen my pain and my shame, and He has rescued me. Jesus is my refuge. He is my place of shelter and my only hope. I can trust Him to protect me". Isaiah 41:13 says, "For I the Lord your God, hold your right hand: I am the Lord who says to you, fear not, I will help you".

Heart to Heart from Pat

You have my book in your hands! When I let that truth grab my head and heart, it blows me away. Think about it, a book just like this changed my entire life forever. A book like this saved my marriage. God used a book like this to call me into full time ministry. I clearly remember that day that I picked up that book about abortion. It was in the summer of 1985. I had just recently given my life to Christ. As I shared earlier, within just a few months God drew my husband and my two sons right behind me. I was immediately passionate about God's word and striving to learn all that I could about living my life for Him. I was also on a bit of a quest to get my husband in "biblical order" when I journeyed out that day to the local Christian bookstore to find some books that would help him learn how to be a better husband. Much to my surprise, standing right smack in the entryway of that bookstore that day that, was a display of books entitled "Will I Cry Tomorrow- Healing Post Abortion Trauma" by Dr. Susan Stanford. The book was Dr. Stanford's story sharing her abortion experience as a young college student. I was brand new in my Christian walk, but I knew immediately in my heart that God had placed that book in my path. A quest to fix my husband was about to rock my world. That was over twenty years ago.

Little did I know that book would change my life! I truly believe that this book is going to change your life as well. You are about to experience an encounter with God just like I did.

I have kept a personal prayer journal for over thirty years. A few years ago, I started to take the time to cover my journals with magazine pictures; scripture and claims of faith for the things going on in my life. I always write the beginning date on the cover as I start the journal and the date I close the last page.

Let me just share a few thoughts from MY JOURNAL written the morning that I arrived in the breathtaking Appalachian Mountains to film the *Surrendering the Secret Bible* study videos in the hot summer of 2007.

"Oh Lord, you have placed me in many amazing spots to write in my journal. I have written in it through many rough growing stages, many life journeys, many praise reports. Salvation is in my journals, new births, deaths, broken friendships, and new friendships. My life, rather my daily morning places are in these pages. But, WOW Lord, these next few days will record a life passage that I believe, aside from my marriage and in my

children being given life, I believe it is one of the reasons that I was born. Your word says that you created, you knit, you fashioned me in my mother's womb that YOU in fact knew the days of my life. Jeremiah tells me that you actually have a plan for me. You knew that I would choose the wild life of youth, Lord. You knew that there was not enough of You in me to direct my paths your way. But even then, you never stopped watching me, I never got away from your grip. In some ways the thought is chilling to my bones. The things that you saw me do Lord, the choices that you saw me make. All the while, instead of turning away in disgust and anger, you — Holy Bridegroom — continued to woo me, to pursue me, to call me. I remember the day that I stopped running, we were not in a pretty place, were we Lord? It was not a pretty scene. But even there, in the depth of my sin, you called into my heart "come away daughter, follow me out of your darkness. Follow my voice and I will lead you to great and mighty places and experiences. To beautiful, majestic views with cool breezes and quiet peace, beyond your dreams!" You did it, Lord! You filled my entire life with great and mighty places and experiences and have blessed me beyond me dreams".

God wants to direct your feet into that same light and peace, complete peace, so that nothing shames you, nothing makes you feel like you have felt as a result of past heartbreaks. He wants you to be free from all insecurity and fear. Through the pages of this book you and I are going to take a journey together, through a process that has set people FREE for over twenty years. I cannot express in mere words all that my heart feels as I greet you. I have prayed for you for so long that I truly feel like I would know you in the grocery store or on the street corner, just by connection of our hearts. I wish that I could be where you are right now so that I could physically wrap my arms around you and calm your fears. This may be the bravest moment in your entire life. I also remember the day that I publicly stepped out as you have stepped out. It was the day that I could hold my secret no longer. The day that I knew that somehow my abortion secret was keeping my walk with God from moving forward, it was keeping me in a place of shame and emptiness that I deeply feared no other person on earth could understand. After all, I had no other choice, I had to do it. I fully believed that I had an abortion for the protection and the benefit of everyone around me. But somehow, deep in my most hidden emotions, something was very wrong.

Something important was missing. My one and only purpose is to encourage you, to love you, to cheer you on. I want to promise you that I am going to walk every step of this journey with you. You are not alone.

We are about to step out together to stand up and shout out to the world, "I AM FREE, I am healed, and I am whole. My God has seen my pain and my shame, and He has rescued me. Jesus is my refuge. He is my place of shelter and my only hope. I can trust Him to protect me". Isaiah 41:13 says "For I the Lord your God, hold your right hand: I am the Lord who says to you, fear not, I will help you"

What more could we ask than that, my friend?

God wants us whole; He wants us healed. Every bit of us, even our secrets. Especially our secrets.

There is a little story called The Runaway Bunny that I have read to all three of my children, now I am reading it to my grandchildren!

Over the next seven chapters, we are going to make believe we are climbing a mountain with the goal of experiencing a glorious view from the top. Now I have got to admit, I am not the most athletic person you will ever meet. I am one of those women who think the best place for hiking boots is in the mall. So if I can do this, you can do this. We just have to remember those words of promise, "I am the Lord who says to you, fear not, I will help you."

I am so proud of you and I want to promise you that if you stick this out and finish this journey, you will get to that virtual mountain peak as a new woman. A woman who fully understands the mighty love that God has for you. He is pursuing you. You are His little girl, you are His daughter, and you are His treasured possession. He knows where you have been, and He knows where He wants to take you!

I will see you again!

A Note about Surrendering the Secret tools Surrendering the Secret

A Surrendered Life is supported by a Bible Study book and coinciding videos that were published by Lifeway called **Surrendering the Secret.** The chapters and video content run parallel in those products and this book and can be used together or independently. Surrendering the Secret is a powerful tool for group or one-on-one Bible study. It has many interactive sessions that will help you process some of what you are reading here and offers some experiential exercises that will support your healing journey. I hope you will grab yourself a brand, new spiral notebook to be your hiking companion as you take this spiritual journey. At the end of each chapter I'll be leaving you with some questions that will help you process what you have read and apply it to your own story. Take some time to allow these questions to stir your memories and you heart enough to begin this journey. This effort will take a lot of trust. I ask you to trust of me as another woman who has been where you have been and where you are going. More importantly it will take trusting God to hold you tight and show you His purpose for leading you to this study.

In addition to the Bible study, we offer a variety of personal healing retreats and online ministry tools. We maintain a website and a resource list of leaders all over the world who have been trained to facilitate Surrendering the Secret Bible studies and healing groups.

NOTE: WE HAVE A SPECIAL COMPANION BOOK FOR MEN

Go to www.surrenderingthesecret.com to find a Surrendering the Secret Bible Study event or leader in your community.

Chapter One JOURNAL TIME

You may or may not be reading this book as someone who has experienced a past abortion.

The journaling suggestions at the end of each chapter will generally reference an abortion decision.

If you have not had an abortion, use this time of reflection to respond to God as He has prompted your heart by what you have read and learned. Substitute your personal story in place of the abortion questions or if you are reading this book to help someone you love, try to complete the answers as best you can.

1. Have you ever experienced a Hagar moment? Has there been a time in your life when running away seemed to be your only option? Journal your experience and God's response.

   _____

   _____

   _____

   _____

   _____

   _____

2. Take some time in a quiet and safe place to pray and ask God to take your hand and walk back with you. Here we go:
   • Where did your abortion/s take place? Write your story.

      _____

      _____

_____

_____

_____

- Who was with you?

_____

_____

- Who knew what was going on for you?

_____

_____

- How did you handle the procedure?

_____

_____

_____

- The aftercare?

_____

_____

_____

- Dealing with your emotions after the procedure was over?

_____

_____

_____

_____

Close your first journal entry with a short prayer asking God to lead you; hold you and direct you into what He wants you to learn from this and begin to show you how you will use your testimony to make Him known in the world.

JOURNAL TIME

_____

_____

_____

_____

_____

_____

_____

_____

_____

_____

_____

_____

_____

_____

_____

_____

_____

_____

_____

_____

_____

_____

_____

_____

2

Sharing the Secret: Going Backwards to Move Forward

Women have what may be the greatest power a human can possess—the power to make a choice to grow and protect a life created in her womb by God or to take action that will terminate that life. Our minds can barely comprehend the reality that two tiny cells can come together in a moment of passion, lust, or ignorance and create a living human being. That new person, if nothing is done to stop it, will draw breath from the minute he or she is born and change the face of the world simply by being. The same is true for the loss of life. Whether or not anyone notices, the loss of a life changes the entire world. The Bible teaches that God created every human being, whether male or female, with a purpose, a destiny, and an assignment.

Next to the impact on the child, the mother suffers the most profound damage from abortion. When a woman chooses abortion a piece of her very self, a piece of her heart dies. That loss cannot be successfully ignored, at least not forever.

No matter how hard she tries to deny the event, at some point, for some reason, the memory returns.

In this chapter we will focus on breaking the power of silence and secrecy. The past has held us captive as a result of a chosen abortion for too long. Let me tell you a story to make a point.

The first time I remember being got caught in a lie I was about eight years old. We were at a cookout on the beach when all of the sudden my sister started crying. Insert the mental image of my most innocent look here. I had NO idea what happened. At least that was the report I gave my mother.

Little did I know that my mother had actually watched me drop a Fiddler Crab into my sisters' swimsuit. The crab had mostly scared my sister, but she acted like I was an ax murderer. I got into some major deep water with my Mom for lying. Paradoxically, however, I was the one who was permanently scarred. Lies hurt others, but like slow-dripping acid they eat us alive from the inside out.

No one has to teach a child to lie. In our fallen world deception is the norm rather than the exception. We've practiced deception since Eve in the garden. People give many excuses. Some people lie for their own selfish gain, but I think most of the time we lie out of fear in attempts to avoid exposure, loneliness, or vulnerability.

Children learn quickly that lying can get them into trouble. They either choose to be more truthful or resort to more lies, sneaking around, or clamming up in silence. As adults we continue in these same patterns. We all have secrets—things we've done we hope no one will ever know about. In the words of Paul, the Apostle, "everyone has sinned; we all fall short of God's glorious standard" (Romans 3:23, NLT).

Every one of us hides something we don't want others to know about—something we're ashamed for them to know. The villain in our life story, the devil, knows that as long as he can keep us bound by our silence and secrets, he can keep us from the freedom God offers. As long as Satan can keep us isolated and separated from others, we automatically remain in bondage. A slogan in recovery programs says it well; we're as sick as our secrets.

As we learn to live in silence and secrecy, many of us end up with a stockpile of hurts that we've buried deep inside ourselves. The only way to overcome and to live free of those hurts is to learn to recognize the lies we've accepted as truth. As we root out each lie, we begin to replace them with the truth. When Jesus said the truth would set us free (John 8:32), He expressed a double meaning. In the ultimate sense we only find freedom in the person of Christ, who is the Truth. In a smaller sense we find freedom bit by bit as we drain lies of their power and expose them to the truth.

Satan uses lies about God, our self-worth, other people, and the world to keep us limping with old infected wounds and trapped in unhealthy ways of living. Culture bombards us with myths and deceptions about sex, love, and life. That's why Jesus spoke strongly about the deceiver who plants so many lies in our world. Jesus said of the devil, "He was a murderer from the beginning and has not stood in the truth, because there is no truth in him. When he tells a lie, he speaks from his own nature, because he is a liar and the father of liars" (John 8:44).

The Apostle Peter knew great failure and shame. After

claiming special commitment and loyalty to Jesus, the brash apostle denied Him only hours later. Peter learned the hard way what he later wrote of the devil, "Be sober! Be on the alert! Your adversary the Devil is prowling around like a roaring lion, looking for anyone he can devour" (1 Peter 5:8, HCSB).

The devil seeks to isolate and slowly destroy you. He is the master deceiver. With the benefit of millennia spent watching human nature, Satan takes advantage of our tendency to try to escape. He knows we will usually run away like Hagar did, rather than making the bold choice to confront our pain.

Unwilling to face our intense emotions or to take responsibility for our actions, we let our burdens become our identities. We accept lies about ourselves and about God. In the process we settle for survival in place of real life. Keeping the secret allows the pain to slowly eat away at us. As a result, we often seek to self-medicate to provide some relief from the pain. Other times we experience the opposite. Because we feel nothing, we use self-destructive behaviors just to feel something.

What about you? What means have you used to escape the pain or to feel through the numbness? Common options include literally medicating with drugs (the most common of which is alcohol), behaviorally medicating through self-destructive behaviors, and in our darkest moments attempts at suicide.

When tempted by these ploys and behaviors we desperately need to remember who our enemy is. Satan strategically uses the wounds in our lives. He strives to distort our identities. He knows our vulnerabilities and takes advantage of our weaknesses. If Satan can keep us feeling worthless, keep us feeling guilty, or keep our minds and hearts under his influence, he can keep us from the glory God intended.

Satan seeks to separate us from the intimacy God wants us to share. That's why the deceiver continually whispers lies about who we are, who God is, God's heart toward us, and the intimacy God wants us to share with Him. Satan employs a three-part strategy to steal, kill, and destroy. The strategy looks like this:

Step One: In the normal course of every person's life, things happen that hurt us, shame us, or cause us to be afraid. The more severe these events, the greater their impact can be. A high-stress pregnancy followed by abortion rates high on any scale of such events.

Step Two: The pain we experience causes a wound. If left untreated with healing or restoration, infection sets in. Infection comes in the form of feelings of rejection; lack of self-worth or worse, feelings of self-hatred. We respond to such feelings with hopelessness, depression, or abusing substances or people.

Step Three: The enemy of life begins to whisper lies in your ear. If you don't have a voice of truth to offset the lies of the evil one, you begin to believe the lies. As time goes by you even begin to speak the lies out as truth: no one loves me; I am a nobody; I am all-alone; I deserve this treatment; it was my fault. Most of all we begin to believe people will never accept me, and God will never forgive me.

All too often Satan succeeds in building in us a distorted view of God and the world. At that point the enemy has won. He then has control of our thoughts. Our thoughts in turn control our actions. We have fallen into his trap.

No wonder Proverbs 4:23 instructs, "above all else, guard your heart, for it is the wellspring of life" (NIV)" Jesus clearly described how powerful the core beliefs of our hearts become in directing our lives and our legacies. "It is what comes from inside that defiles you. For from within, out of a person's heart, come evil thoughts" (Mark 7:20-21).

The battle of life happens mostly inside you and me, in our minds. We have an enemy who fights dirty, and our secrets give him ammunition. He proves more than happy to use our secrets against us. So, one of the most practical things any of us can do is to break the silence. When we open our secrets to the light of shared truth, we literally take out of the devil's hands the stick he has been using to beat us black and blue.

So how do we break the silence and get free? How do we overcome years and years of enemy strongholds over our thoughts, beliefs and lives? The answer scares us terribly. We need to tell our story.

We need to speak out the hurts and pain. We need to expose the darkness to the light. This step has a purpose far beyond reopening old wounds. In an amazing way, honesty builds community. God never intended us to struggle alone. People need each other, and we were designed for strong relationships. Amazing things occur when two or more people grasp hands and hearts and share their pain together. God is in their midst. He does amazing things with those who are humble and open to His supernatural surgery of the heart. Through God's power we find recovery, freedom, and healing.

Solomon, the wisest human king of ever, described our need for each other in the Book of Ecclesiastes. He said a person without a companion experiences "no end" of struggles. "Two are better than one because they have a good reward for their efforts. For if either fall, his companion can lift him up; but pity the one who falls without another to lift him up. Also, if two lie down together, they can keep warm; but how can one person alone keep warm? And if somebody overpowers one person, two can resist him. A cord of three strands is not easily broken" (Ecclesiastes 4:9-12, HCSB).

Everyone needs someone we trust and with whom we can share our story. We need someone who will listen and not judge. We need someone who will keep our story confidential and who will pray with and for us. This need isn't limited to those of us with abortion in our past, but the more shameful our past seems the more desperate the need.

Because the very thought of surrendering our secret shame frightens us so, we need to consider what disclosure does and does not mean. I am not suggesting that transparency means telling everyone everything. Healthy boundaries mean we disclose ourselves appropriately to the right people in the right way at the right time. It most definitely does not mean we open ourselves to unsafe people.

A daunting problem for many of us was how to find the safe person or group where we could share our pain. Sometimes we don't even know what a safe person looks like. As someone said we need someone who will know all about us and love us still. We need others who will both love us unconditionally and tell us the truth.

If you already have that kind of relationship, you're a fortunate person. You're in a very distinct and blessed minority. Many people desperately long for such deep relationships. If you are like most of us, you will have to seek out that kind of support.

Many of us have found great benefit from seeking a safe place to share our experiences through specialized groups outside of our regular friends. A homogenous group of people who have shared similar experiences can hear our story with understanding. In a purely pragmatic sense, openness with strangers can simply be easier. Many churches and local pregnancy centers offer counseling and support both for men and women. You may want to join a Surrendering the Secret Bible Study. Go to www.surrenderingthesecret.com to find more about the Bible study and possible groups in your area.

Those of us who have an abortion in our past often find absolutely terrifying the thought of being found out. We probably chose abortion in the first place to keep a secret. We feared the pregnancy would be discovered. Fear continues to be one reason many women and men have guarded their secret for years. In the process we've fallen for a great a deception.

Who do we really protect by holding onto the secret? We cover up the deceiver's lie that abortion doesn't hurt us. We reinforce society's belief that the choice doesn't hurt women. Remaining silent keeps us in the darkness of the lie, but freedom comes in exposing it.

Please understand God's desire is not to expose you, leaving you feeling alone and vulnerable. Rather God knows that your confession exposes the darkness to the light. Once in the light God can do His healing work. You have a protecting and caring Father who covers His children with grace, not shame. Be courageous; under the protection of God, expose the enemy.

I knew I had a ways to go. I'd come to the end of myself and given my life to Jesus in a big, fat mess. My marriage had been in shambles, my kids were being thrown back and forth between my husband and me. I had a lot to get right. In the middle of these present problems I couldn't imagine why God would have me concentrating on something that had happened seven years earlier. Weren't we supposed to forget the past and concentrate on the future?

I had never talked to anyone about my abortion. It was secret. Something I barely remembered myself. Yet I had no doubt God was leading me. I called one of my new Bible study girlfriends and asked her to meet me for lunch.

My heart pounded in my chest and my head was spinning. My friend Ann, with her sparkling smile, was bounding toward me from the tearoom parking lot. No getting away this time, I was too late to duck. Ann instinctively reached for my hands as I began to tremble, and tears ran down my cheeks. I had never been so scared in my life.

Ann was my new best friend. She first approached me at the church ladies' retreat. She had invested in me, pulling me into her circle of beautiful, godly women, and coaching me in my new walk with God. Ann was the person who taught me how to pray out loud. She was the one who planted within me a hunger for the Bible and a desire for intimacy with God. She continued to walk with me step-by-step through the metamorphosis into my new life in Jesus.

In the few months that had passed since I surrendered my life to God at that ladies' retreat my life had turned around so beautifully. My marriage, my children, even my music had been transformed by the new life Jesus offers. My spirit and emotions had gone from depression to hopeful. Little did I suspect that this incredible walk into new life with God would lead me to a crossroad where I found myself face-to-face with a dark secret from my old life. Not only had I hidden this secret from the world, I had stuffed it so deep inside that I was hiding it from myself.

As I clutched Ann's hands that day at the tearoom, I felt like my newly found peace and joy was about to be demolished, but I knew God was asking me to surrender my secret, just as He'd asked that I surrender my life to Him.

Although I was dreading it, I had to tell Ann about my abortion. The secret swelled so fiercely in my heart that I was about to burst. Turmoil and panic gripped my chest because I had no idea what Ann would say or how exposing this dark part of my past would affect our friendship. Ann and all my new friends at church seemed so godly and good. What would they think of me? What would they think about the awful thing I had done?

You've made a huge step by reading this far. I'll share more or what happened later. For now, let me use my friend Sheri's words.

She shares hope through her story.

> *"I remember being in your shoes not so long ago and thinking that this was not going to work. Opening up would be impossible for anyone who hurt like I did over my abortion. It was just too personal. The amazing thing I discovered through the process was that I was*

not alone in my pain and sorrow. The decision to heal must come from your heart; no one can force you into anything. Start courageously and finish strong!"

Your Sister in Christ,

Sheri

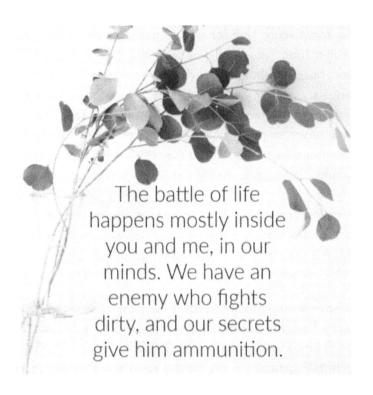

The battle of life happens mostly inside you and me, in our minds. We have an enemy who fights dirty, and our secrets give him ammunition.

Heart to Heart from Pat

Wow! This has been another tough chapter challenge hasn't it? Not only have you picked this book up and confronted a secret that has been hidden deep in your heart but now you have spent some time looking at how that secret has stolen freedom from you. You have seen how the "Father of Lies", Satan, has used that painful choice to take your own life in so many ways. Over the past twenty years that I have been ministering to women who have been sold the lie of abortion, I have never stopped being shocked or heartbroken at the things that women are told. At the crisis pregnancy center that I founded in Tampa, we receive close thousands of contacts each year from woman who are facing an unwanted to unplanned pregnancy. They come to us having heard all sorts of false information about the development of their unborn child, the simplicity of the abortion procedure and the ease of their recovery.

You have learned many statistics this past week, some coming directly from the abortion industry itself. You looked at some factual information that women need to know but have no one to tell them. If we are bound up in our abortion secrets, how will women ever hear the truth about the pain and horror of an abortion procedure? How will they hear the truth about the so-called "quick recovery" that follows abortion? How will they know what God says about abortion if the church is silent in our wounds?

I was so very ignorant of any of those things when I chose to have an abortion. All I Could think about at that time was my shame and my need for a quick fix that no one would ever have to know about.

At the end of chapter one you had some questions to ask yourself and to ask God about how you are feeling after all that you have been reading. It is one thing to remember some of the details of our own abortion experience but quite another to actually share them with someone else. I cannot even count all of the women that I have ministered post abortion healing to over the past many years, but every single time, I think of all the women and all of the babies that have been damaged and destroyed by this destructive choice. You have studied a new term called Post Abortion Trauma and seen the many ways that choosing an abortion can affect your life even beyond the loss of your unborn child. I am certain that you have identified many things that you have experienced firsthand over the past years. This is a difficult journey that will lead not only to your freedom but to the freedom that truth will bring to many other women and young girls who are all at risk for these lies.

In the next chapter, I will share a poem that I wrote shortly after reading what God had to say about the unborn child in Psalm 139. I am sure that you will relate to some of the feeling that I express in my poem as similar to your own. That poem was written in 1986, just two short years after I came to know the Lord. God has done so much in my life since those days. He has actually used my pain to minister to others. He has revealed His healing love in my life, and He has set me on a course that seems to get richer and richer with each new day. As I have studied Psalm 139, it has become one of my favorite scriptures as I hear it not only for my precious lost child, but also for myself.

Allow me, if you will, to pray over you as you continue reading.

Thank you, my Lord, that you have searched my dear sister and you know her. You know when she sits down and when she stands, you understand her thoughts from far away. You, Lord, observe her travels and her rest and are aware of all of her ways. Before a word is on her tongue Lord, you know it. You have encircled her and placed your hand upon her. This extraordinary knowledge is beyond our ability to understand. Where can she go to escape your spirit Lord? Where can she flee from your presence? IF she goes to heaven you are there, if she makes her bed in the depths you are there. If she rises on the wings of the dawn, if she settles on the far side of the sea, even there your hand will guide her and your right hand will hold her fast.

If she says surely darkness will hide me, and the light become night around me, even the darkness will not be dark to you, the night will shine like the day, for darkness is light to you Lord. For you most high God have knit her together in her mother's womb, she is fearfully and wonderfully made, your works are wonderful. She knows that full well. Her frame was not hidden from you when she was made in the secret places, when she was woven together in the depths of the earth; your eyes saw her unformed body.

All the days ordained for her were written in your book before even one of them came to be. How precious are your thoughts O God, how vast is the sum of them, were I to count them they would outnumber the grains of sand. When she wakes up Lord, she is still with you. Oh Lord, if only you would slay the wicked and the bloodthirsty men, they speak of you with evil intent and misuse your name. She hates those who hate you O Lord, search her O Lord, see if there is any offensive way in her and lead her in the way everlasting.

Thank you, Holy God. Amen

God is leading you today sweet friend, as the Psalm says, He is watching you and leading you. Trust Him.

Chapter Two JOURNAL TIME

Take some time to think and pray about who knows about your abortion. Are they someone you can trust to share this experience? WARNING—I strongly recommend that you do NOT contact an old boyfriend or ex-spouse during this process unless God gives you clear direction to do that and it is confirmed by mature Christina leaders. Ask God for direction and leading towards a Christian friend, spouse or ministry leader. If you are not ready for that step, take the time to write your story out in your journal. Last chapters' questions should have gotten you started in remembering the story of your abortion experience. If you have never had a past abortion, take this time to understand the difficulty of this step by considering a past "secret" of your own.

Take your time; ask God to help you; and allow our online community to be a resource and support to you.

Here are some additional questions to stir your thoughts and to help you "Share Your Story" either in person or in writing.

- What were your life circumstances and relationships like at the time of your abortion?

- Was there anyone in your life you felt you could completely trust?
- When or how did the idea of abortion come to mind? What other options did you consider?
- Describe your abortion experience.
- Share thoughts and feelings you recall before, during, and after the abortion.
- What about you changed the day of the abortion?

Who do we really protect by holding onto the secret?

JOURNAL TIME

_____

_____

_____

_____

_____

_____

_____

_____

_____

_____

_____

_____

_____

_____

_____

_____

_____

_____

_____

_____

_____

_____

_____

_____

_____

JOURNAL TIME

3

What is the Truth?

Abortion advocates present it to women as a quick fix, an easy out, an over-in-a-minute answer for an unplanned, unwanted pregnancy. When a woman enters an abortion clinic she is in the passion of crisis. Panic, shame or fear often overrules facts. Women who choose abortion have been compared to an animal willing to chew its own leg off to free itself from the jaws of a trap. I know, I am one of those women.

After discovering what God had to say about life and abortion and during my own walk to healing, I wrote the following poem:

> I knew before they spoke it,
> As women often do,
> That a life had formed inside me
> Though I prayed it not be true.

In an instant, I was not alone,
fear stood by constantly,
it attacked my thoughts in dark, black moods,
How could this have happened to me?

I do not want this baby
there is no other way; "GET RID OF IT"
were words I heard.
the price seemed a small to pay.

The whiteness of the ceiling,
bright lights and sharp cold air
are vivid in my memories,
I never knew I'd care. Years went past with only fleeting
thoughts of
what "it" might have been.
It never even dawned on me that
murder is a sin.

It never seemed to me that way,
until one awful night,
a nightmare broke into my sleep,
I screamed and cried with fright.

I could see the Lord beside me,
by that table, in that place,
I saw His eyes, and heard His voice,
and tears streamed down His face.

In a broken voice He said to me,
"My daughter, tell me why?
I worked with love to make that child
for you to let it die."

Since that meeting with the Lord,
He's healed my wounds and sins,
but I'll never be completely healed
until ABORTION ENDS.
- Pat Layton, 1986

44

In Chapter two we discussed the process of deception Satan uses to rob us of freedom and an abundant life. The Bible calls the devil the father of lies. Satan continues to pour his twisted deceptions into our world. God knows how lies provide Satan his best ammunition. When we fall for and then perpetrate deceit, bit-by-bit we take on the character of the evil one.

God hates lies for at least two reasons. They represent the very opposite of His character, and they hurt those He loves. Scripture makes clear God's opinion of all things false, "Lying lips are detestable to the LORD, but faithful people are His delight" (Proverbs 12:22, HCSB). Proverbs 6:16-19 says the Lord hates six things, "haughty eyes, a lying tongue, hands that shed innocent blood, a heart that devises wicked schemes, feet that are quick to rush into evil, a false witness who pours out lies and a man who stirs up dissension among brothers" (Proverbs 6:16-19, NIV).

God didn't put those statements in His Word to make us miserable or to control us. He seeks to guide and to protect us by setting boundaries for our own good. We learned from John 10:32 that the truth will set us free. No lie ever has or ever will bring freedom. Whether people lie for their own gain, to protect themselves, or because they have personally bought into the deception, lies cause serious damage. The power of a lie bears fruit when we will act on it as truth.

Lies have eroded truth many places in our world. We have built a world culture very much like the one described in Jeremiah 9 "They make ready their tongue like a bow, to shoot lies... They go from one sin to another; they do not acknowledge me, declares the LORD. Everyone has to be on guard against his friend. Don't trust any brother, for every brother will certainly deceive, and every friend spread slander. Each one betrays his friend; no one tells the truth." (Jeremiah 9:3-5, HCSB).

To find freedom we must build a microcosm of truth out of this world of deception. We begin that process in our relationship to God and with at least one trustworthy fellow human.

If like me you face the aftermath of an abortion, consider the circumstances that led to your original decision. As you made your abortion decision, what messages did you hear? Did those closest to you tell you it was okay, that it was your only choice? Did billboards, Internet or media articles influence you? As part of healing we must look at what we believed when we chose abortion and begin to understand some of the effects that may have followed.

Statistics tell us that most abortions occur on women between eighteen and twenty-four years of age. We are exploring many of our values and moral codes in that period of life. For me, it was a season of making choices and practicing behaviors that I never truly choose, but more accurately, I followed. Even when we chose abortion later in life, women indicate having made the decision outside or in spite of, deeply held moral values and beliefs.

For many women and men, the first emotion after an abortion is immediate relief that they're no longer burdened with the unwanted pregnancy. Research indicates, however, that this short-lived relief is frequently replaced by guilt, shame, secrecy, sadness, and regret. This unexpected reaction to an abortion decision is commonly referred to as post-abortion trauma. Approximately 40% of post-abortive women experience intense traumatic responses, but statistics reveal that 80% will experience some level of symptoms. Some psychologists believe the statistic is actually as high as 100% of women who suffer some measure of trauma.

Review these alarming (albeit every changing) statistics on the negative effects of abortion:[1]

· 92% of women who've had abortions experience emotional deadening
· 63% experience denial
· 58% battle nightmares
· 86% experience anger or rage
· 56% develop suicidal feelings
· 86% fear others finding out
· 53% engage in drug abuse
· 82% experience intense feelings of loneliness or isolation
· 39% have eating disorders

In past years, the Alan Guttmacher Institute, a division of Planned Parenthood, has presented statistics that 43% of American women will have an abortion by age forty-five. The institute says half of all pregnancies in the U.S. are unintended; out of those, four in ten will end in abortion. In the U.S. alone, more than 1.5 million abortions are performed each year, making abortion one of the most common elective surgical procedures performed on women today.[2]

The same statistical research indicates some reasons women respond to the question, "Why do Women Get Abortions":[3]

· 75% said their baby would interfere with their lives
· 66% said they couldn't afford a child
· 50% didn't want to be a mother at the time

· 4% had a doctor who said their health would worsen with the baby

· 1% had a fetal abnormality

· 1% were victims of rape or incest

The effects reported by men whose wife or girlfriend had an abortion are not entirely different from the aftershocks suffered by women. In the late Guy Condon's heartfelt book *"Fatherhood Aborted"*, he lists the following symptoms of male post-abortion trauma.

You have difficulty with commitment.
You dodge authority.
You have no solid sense of authority.
You work to impress moral leaders.
You keep women at bay.
You have trouble bonding.
You fear impending tragedy.
You don't own your mistakes.
You feel inadequate as a leader.

Where do we find TRUTH?

Obviously, abortion brings unexpected results. Both women and men discover the painful and damaging consequences only after the fact. If neither media nor medical professionals provide the complete truth, how are Christians to know what abortion truly costs? How does abortion really impact a society or culture? Understanding the statistics along with the truth and direction found in the Word of God, we can make an informed decision concerning abortion.

Considering the statistics above, abortion clearly does not represent the best choice, the only choice, or the choice without complications. It runs opposite to the value the Word of God places on a human life.

Heated debate rages about when life begins. The very question comes from our desire to justify abortion. The idea that life begins at birth or somewhere in the gestation process gives abortion advocates what they believe to be intellectual grounds to justify the procedure. However, the idea violates both science and Scripture.

The scientific facts about the beginning of life simply show that life does not begin in the birth process at all. Life clearly began long ago. Creationists believe life began with God's work. Evolutionists believe life began through random processes. Both positions absolutely agree about a key point. Life began in the distant past and is passed on from one generation to the next. Once we recognize that simple fact, no question exists about when life is passed from parents to child.

The Bible doesn't say a great deal about when life begins, probably because the question is so very artificial. The writers of Scripture could never have conceived of modern attitudes about a baby as a burden rather than a blessing. When the Bible does speak of pre-natal life the message is clear; the Psalmist said, "Oh yes, you shaped me first inside, then out; you formed me in my mother's womb. I thank you, High God—you're breathtaking! Body and soul, I am marvelously made! I worship in adoration—what a creation! You know me inside and out, you know every bone in my body; You know exactly how I was made, bit-by-bit, how I was sculpted from nothing into something. Like an open book, you watched me grow from conception to birth; all the stages of my life were spread out before you, the days of my life all prepared before I'd even lived one day" (Psalm 139:13-16, The Message).

I stated earlier that a large percentage of abortions occur to young women. I was an exception; I had given birth to my first child at eighteen. Years later, when faced with a choice for abortion with my second pregnancy, the stage of development of my unplanned baby was the last of my concerns. I never studied nor really considered the development process of my unborn child. I was more worried about what I would do with a born child than spending any time learning the stages of an unborn one.

I have counseled thousands of women over the past twenty-five years and have rarely encountered one who allowed her thoughts to take the path of considering the development of the baby. Few of us have had the opportunity to voice our thoughts and questions. Our society considers such concerns untouchable. We can't understand the amazing elements of creating a person's soul, but the physical development of the baby is beyond what most of us would imagine:

· At 21 days the heart begins to beat
· At 40 days brain waves can be detected by an EEG
· At 6 to 7 weeks the baby can respond to touch
· At eight weeks he or she has every required body part
· The duration of the pregnancy is for growth of the fully developed body parts

Though many people consider such concerns off limits, we can't escape thinking about child development. Whatever they may say, the truth is, we do think about it. We wonder what our child might have been. We imagine what his or her life might have been like. God knows what our unborn babies were like in every cell of their bodies. He knows what the child would have looked like at twelve years old or as a young adult. Life does not begin with the first breath or the first heartbeat. It begins in the heart and mind of God before conception. Women have been endowed with the incredible ability and opportunity to give life to eternal souls created in the image of God!

As we acknowledge the choice to end our baby's life, we feel alone in our thoughts and feelings. Who would understand such dreary thinking? Who would allow such wonderings or questions? The act of abortion is not openly discussed so who would allow our mothers hearts to wander into such questions? When a woman loses a child to miscarriage or stillbirth, even then, she feels discomfort in such a discussion. How much greater is the secret issue of abortion. However, I have good news for you my sister, someone does understand.

Look with me at some other parts of Psalm 139:

> O LORD, you have searched me and you know me.
> You know when I sit and when I rise; you perceive my thoughts from afar.
> You discern my going out and my lying down; you are familiar with all my ways.
> Before a word is on my tongue you know it completely, O LORD.
> You hem me in—behind and before; you have laid your hand upon me.
> Such knowledge is too wonderful for me, too lofty for me to attain.
> Where can I go from your Spirit? Where can I flee from your presence?
> If I go up to the heavens, you are there; if I make my bed in the depths, you are there.
> If I rise on the wings of the dawn, if I settle on the far side of the sea,
> even there your hand will guide me, your right hand

will hold me fast.

If I say, "Surely the darkness will hide me and the light become night around me,"

even the darkness will not be dark to you; the night will shine like the day, for darkness is as light to you. (Psalm 139:1-12, NIV)

Nothing is hidden from God's sight. He is with you during the darkest, loneliest, and most difficult times of your life. God sees with complete clarity in the darkness of your soul and your deep secrets. God never leaves you.

Nothing is hidden from God's sight. He is with you during the darkest, loneliest, and most difficult times of your life.

Many men and women report feelings of guilt, shame, depression, regret, and anger over their abortion. Others describe struggling with feelings of unworthiness, fear, numbness, and lack of trust. Many turn to substance abuse and other destructive behavior as a result. Perhaps some of these emotions or actions seem familiar. You may have never connected these dots and realized that your feelings could be a result of your abortion. Keeping us from understanding the cause and effect represents just another way the enemy deceives post-abortive women—and men.

In another place the Psalmist wrote, "When I kept silent about my sin, my body wasted away through my groaning all day long. For day and night your hand was heavy upon me, my vitality was drained away as with the fever heat of summer" (Psalm 32:3-4, NASB). Praise God, however, the Psalmist didn't describe only the problem. He continued to the healing solution, "I acknowledged my sin to you and my iniquity I did not hide. I said, 'I will confess my transgressions to the LORD: and you forgave the guilt of my sin'" (Psalm 32: 5, NASB).

According to this passage, when we stay silent regarding out sin, our bodies waste away, and our energy literally drains away. Secrets can play havoc on a person's physical, emotional, mental, and spiritual well-being. We can't allow ourselves to stop with that loss. God wants to heal our hearts and use our stories to help others. Confession leads to forgiveness and peace.

Several times we've looked at God's promises of truth, hope, and redemption. The other remedies we've tried to relieve the pain of our abortions trap us in dark places. We've tried self-destructive remedies like drugs, alcohol, and meaningless relationships. You may be reading this book because you've already discovered you can't find your way out of those dark places alone.

Rescue begins when we acknowledge that we are powerless to heal our lives on our own. Only the Savior can rescue, re-create, and restore us from the inside out. We've discussed how, if we want to experience healing, we must be willing to trust Jesus to take us on the unfamiliar and risky path to it.

Heart to Heart from Pat

The enemy knows where we are vulnerable, and he knows what it will take to set us free. He does not like truth, he does not like freedom. John 8:44 says "the devil was a murderer from the beginning, not holding to the truth, for there is no truth in him. When he lies, he speaks his native language, for he is a liar, and the father of lies". Just a few verses ahead of that scripture in John, Jesus Himself tells us "when you know the truth, the truth will set you free". It is His only reason for drawing you to this study. It is not to shame you, but to cut away the shame from you. To help you see the truth about abortion so that you can be free from its grip on your past.

There was a woman who Jesus once met at a well where he went to rest and get a drink of water. The story is found in the book of John, chapter 4. The woman, who had also come to the well for water, had a life changing encounter with Jesus as he confronted her secrets that He knew about her past, he knew about the guys and the marriages and the abuse and the load that she carried deep in her heart!! We know that Jesus came to well with no burdens, no loads because she curiously asked him, how are you going to get water, you have nothing to put it in. She on the other hand, was loaded down with a big heavy jar for her to put her water in. As we take our next step towards the mountain peak, you may feel a lot like her. She came to that same well, hot, tired and loaded down with burdens that she was very tired of carrying. I know that you have come to this place with a heavy load, a load that our Lord does not want you to carry.

My family has a dirty old hiking backpack that we have used for a lot of years. We normally have some things in here that we need for a good long hike, some water, some refreshments, and a map!! But sometimes after a few uses we begin to gather some stuff that makes that backpack heavier. This healing journey is a lot like a mountain climb in many ways, mainly the fact that there is a marvelous destination and it is well worth the climb. This chapter gives us the opportunity to dump some stuff out of our backpack that will slow us down, keeping us from getting to the top.

Back to our Bible study, after her encounter with Jesus, the woman's response to his knowledge of her past failure and shame, was freedom, instead of a slow heavy walk, she ran back to town telling people, "He knew me, He knew my sin, He knew my secrets...He is the Messiah". Her load was lighter; her run was swift and free! Jesus is your messiah as well. He wants the same freedom for you today as you start this healing journey.

The very first time that I ever told the story of my abortion experience out loud was with my dear friend Ann. I am all too familiar with the panic in your heart right now, with the sick feeling in your stomach. You may have been holding onto this secret for ten years like I had — or for you it may even be twenty years, or it may have been last year! The choice to have an abortion is sold to women as the great escape, the easy out, the quick fix and sometimes, the only choice. But we know differently don't we. We know that nothing can compare to the intentional destruction of our own children. No one, who has not been there, could completely ever understand the shame and loss that we feel. How very difficult it is to even speak the words that tell the story. No one but Jesus! God wants to help you. The Bible says in James 5:16 "confess your sins to each other and pray for each other so that you can be healed." Isn't God amazing? He knows how much we need one another.

God will help you when the time comes to share at the right time with the right person or people. When I shared with my friend Ann, she had not had an abortion in her past, she has never heard an abortion story and she had no idea what I was going to share with her but I can tell you that God Himself filled her heart and her mouth and she easily and sincerely embraced me and spoke words of love and support and truth to me in those moments. Her Godly response changed my life. I am praying that every person who reads this book and needs someone they can trust to share with finds that person, but I can assure you that the Surrendering the Secret leadership team is here for you. Contact us through our website or Facebook and we will help you process your story.

Chapter Three JOURNAL TIME

Take some time for prayer and reflection. Ask God to help you get a deeper insight into all you have considered in this section. You may have encountered a lot of new information. You may never have envisioned aborted children as "being knit together by God." Give God time to show you His heart for you as you proceed towards the complete healing He wants for His daughters. God may show you how you have allowed the enemy's lies to push you around. He also may show you how you have been affected by the lie when faced with it by well-meaning friends, family, the church, or the media.

God created us in His image (Gen 1:27) with the freedom of choice. Since the moment Adam and Eve chose to disobey God, the world has been anything but paradise. Our freedom to choose has destroyed life across the ages, but God willingly created us with the freedom to make our own decisions. We always have free choice, but choices always have consequences. Before entering the Promised Land, Moses challenged the Israelites saying, "Today I have given you the choice between life and death, between blessings and curses. Now I call on heaven and earth to witness the choice you make. Oh, that you would choose life, so that you and your descendants might live" (Deuteronomy 30:19, NLT).

Will you reject the past with its shame, curses, and death, choosing instead the path to life, freedom and blessing with Jesus? Will you choose life?

This can be an overwhelming chapter. You may be reading these truths for the first time. New feelings may be starting to stir inside you, and you may begin to feel angry. That is to be expected. The next chapter will deal with the emotion of anger, as the post-abortive woman manifests it. As you reflect on your journey, let me suggest some clarifying questions to ask yourself. These questions will help to think through aspects of your situation.

Questions to Consider: Regarding the Father of the Child

What part did your relationship with your child's father play in your decision?

_____

_____

_____

Was he involved? _____

Did he know about your choice? _____

If you were the father, was the choice made without your input? _____

If you contributed to the choice, do you feel that you had all of the truth when you made your abortion decision?

_____

When you ask God a question, expect His Spirit to respond to your heart. Be careful not to rush it or manufacture an answer. Don't turn the Bible into a reference book or spiritual encyclopedia. Just pose the question to God and wait on Him. The litmus test for anything we hear from God is alignment with the Bible as our ultimate truth source.

The following questions ask you to look into your heart and

consider with brutal honesty your deepest feelings and beliefs. Remember, our behaviors are the best indicators of what we really believe in our innermost being (Psalm 51:6.) Be sure to capture your insights and feelings.

Questions to Consider: As to Myself

What lies do I still hold onto that prevent me from feeling the full impact of my decision to end my child's life?

_____

_____

_____

_____

What lies about abortion do I continue to hold?

_____

_____

_____

Questions to Consider: of God

Your Word says that you can see me, Lord. Why do You allow something like abortion to be available to us when You know how much it will hurt?

Why didn't you stop me?

Where were You?

Take some time for personal reflection and inventory of how you are doing at this point in your journey.

What are your concerns? Fears? Prayers?

_____

_____

_____

_____

_____

_____

_____

_____

_____

_____

_____

_____

_____

_____

_____

_____

_____

_____

_____

4

Drinking Poison

When we take the time to understand the truth about abortion, feelings of anger often result. Truth means facing the facts about the millions upon millions who are affected, the millions upon millions who are permanently scarred. Facing the truth about abortion forces us to understand how many sisters, friends, aunts, cousins and daughters endure the heartbreak and shame of abortion. Truth means we shed the false comfort of believing what we wish were real.

Nothing Was True

I struggled to open my eyes. Although I could hear soft whispers of unknown words in the room, I could not move my body or speak past the tube running down my throat. I couldn't remember where I was or how I got there. Within moments, I would wish I had not awakened at all.

My newly wedded husband and my parents stood

numbly at the foot of my hospital bed, as I was struggling regain consciousness.

As tiny bits of my body and my mind began to regain feeling, a flood of anger rushed into each space. Now, I remember.

The people at the hospital said that the whole procedure would be over in thirty minutes. They said I would be picking up my five-year-old son from school that afternoon. They said a few aspirin would do the trick after the procedure.

Nothing they said was true.

My abortion was supposed to be a three-hour break in my busy day, allowing me to go on with my life by noon. Instead, I had an allergic reaction to the anesthesia they used to put me to sleep and they had to put me on a respirator to keep me alive. By noon I was still unable to breathe on my own, much less pick up my son from school. My new husband was forced to call on my parents to do that for us. Of course, after picking our son up from school, my parents had rushed to the hospital.

The people at the clinic had said no one would even have to know. They said there was "no need to worry" about the fever and the cramps that lasted five days after I went home from the hospital. As I grew worse, they changed their minds and said, "During the emergency we encountered during your first procedure, parts of the fetus were left behind. We will need to repeat the abortion procedure."

I never even thought about the word "fetus" until they

said it. After that, all I could think was "baby." My baby. "Parts" left behind? Which "parts?" The heart? The hands? The parts of a boy or of a girl? My God, which parts?

Nothing they said was true.

Looking into the numbers and examining the intentional strategies of abortion proponents causes women to begin to think about other people who may have been involved in their abortion decision. You may be tempted to feel that even reading this book is complicating your life, not making it easier. You've had to draw on immense courage to revisit the past and face some difficult truths. Right about now you are probably wondering *why am I doing this to myself?*

Please don't give up. Keep reading. It is costly to go back, but it is more costly not to go back. Your freedom is worth it. The freedom and truth that you will find in your search could save a life and will definitely change yours.

The Power of Anger

Anger is an extremely powerful emotion. Most of the time we view it as a negative part of ourselves that should be denied or at least controlled. The truth is God created all our emotions for our benefit—including anger. However, when we don't use emotions properly, we can do a great deal of damage both to others and ourselves. Let's talk about anger, the good, the bad and the ugly.

The Bible has much to say about how to handle our emotions the right way. A verse in Ephesians shows us that anger isn't necessarily a sin. It instructs us to lay aside falsehood and, "speak the truth each of you with his neighbor, for we are all

members of one another. Be angry, and yet do not sin"
(Ephesians 4:25-26, NASB).

What? Did the Bible just give us permission to be angry?
Anger is a God given emotion and is not a sin. How we deal
with our anger may be either wholesome or sinful. Anger
becomes dangerous and destructive when we react to it in
ways that hurt others and ourselves.

Think of unmanaged anger as being like the acid in your car
battery. In the right container and used for the right purpose,
the acid provides power to start your car. In the wrong
container anger becomes corrosive and destructive of
whatever it contacts.

God gave you the ability to feel anger as a motive force.
When we encounter false and hurtful things, anger motivates
us to change them. But anger has a short useful shelf life. If
we hold on to our anger for weeks, months, or years then it
can overtake our lives and consume who we are. As the anger
corrodes our soul, every thought, every action can become
motivated by anger and the resulting bitterness. The person
God created us to be ends up buried deep beneath anger,
with resentment and bitterness piled on top.

The words, "be angry" in Ephesians 4:26 is in the Greek
imperative tense used for commands or direct instructions.
Shockingly, to those of us who have learned to deny and stuff
our anger, in this passage God actually commands us to be
angry. Two excellent examples in the Bible illustrate God's
command.

Moses was an Israelite slave in Egypt whom God miraculously
spared from slaughter through his mother's great courage
and sacrifice. God raised Moses into a position of great

influence in the Pharaoh's household, but the events of one day changed all that. The Book of Exodus tells the story as follows:

Years later, after Moses had grown up, he went out to his own people and observed their forced labor. He saw an Egyptian beating a Hebrew, one of his people. Looking all around and seeing no one, he struck the Egyptian dead and hid him in the sand. The next day he went out and saw two Hebrews fighting. He asked the one in the wrong, "Why are you attacking your neighbor?" "Who made you a leader and judge over us?" the man replied. "Are you planning to kill me as you killed the Egyptian?" Then Moses became afraid and thought: What I did is certainly known. When Pharaoh heard about this, he tried to kill Moses. But Moses fled from Pharaoh and went to live in the land of Midian. (Exodus 2:11-15, HCSB)

Moses became angry when he saw how Egyptians were treating the Hebrews—his people. His anger was justified. What was not justified was allowing that anger to spill over in killing the Egyptian. Moses sin was not being angry but committing murder. His response to anger was not healthy or constructive in solving Israel's problem. It actually made things worse and resulted in Moses having to flee the country. Moses should have and could have channeled his anger in more constructive ways. For example, Fredrick Douglass was a slave in the pre-Civil War south. After escaping slavery, he became an abolitionist leader who as an author and orator greatly influenced the efforts to outlaw slavery. Douglass channeled his anger in constructive ways. The result contributed to freedom for millions and changed history.

Jesus provides us another example of anger in the Bible.

When He saw how temple businessmen were cheating and extorting people who came to the temple to worship God, Jesus too demonstrated anger.

Jesus entered the Temple and began to drive out all the people buying and selling animals for sacrifice. He knocked over the tables of the moneychangers and the chairs of those selling doves. He said to them, "The Scriptures declare, 'My Temple will be called a house of prayer,' but you have turned it into a den of thieves!" (Matthew 21:10-13, NLT)

Jesus responded differently to anger. Jesus did not destructively hurt anyone. Yes, he made a mess, but Jesus channeled His anger for a purpose. He was angry at how the people of Jerusalem were treating the temple. They had turned a holy place into a market, a place where people were taking advantage of others, and a place of business, not worship. His actions were instructive and corrective. In the process He definitely ruffled some feathers.

Of course, as the Son of God, Jesus was better able to judge the degree of action to take with His anger. I'm not recommending we take a bullwhip to the person in the overpriced kiosk at the mall. The offense Jesus faced was serious. His reaction was measured and proportional.

From Jesus' cleansing the temple we can see that physically expressing anger can be justified under some circumstances. Such righteous anger must be neither a means to selfish gain nor a way to hurt someone. Acting on anger may be justified when it results in a change and makes the world a better place. Godly anger aligns us with the emotion God feels when people are abused.

As women who have chosen abortion, we often face a great

deal of anger. The challenge is to sort through that anger and express it in healthy and constructive ways. For each of us dealing with anger will be different, but it has some common elements.

Godly anger aligns
us with the emotion
God feels when
people are abused.

To Implode or Explode?

Are you an imploder or an exploder when it comes to anger? Dr. Gary Chapman describes two unhealthy ways of managing anger, holding it in or expressing it with aggressive behaviors. Implosive anger is internalized anger that we never outwardly express. You might hear, "I'm not angry, just frustrated" or "I'm not mad, just disappointed" as two common expressions of an imploder.

Since so many of us have been taught to deny our anger, we do well to examine the previously cited Bible passage from Ephesians a little more closely. The Apostle Paul wrote:

Therefore, laying aside falsehood, speak the truth each one of you with his neighbor, for we are members of one another. Be angry, and yet do not sin; do not let the sun go down on your anger, and do not give the devil an opportunity. He who steals must steal no longer; but rather he must labor, performing with his own hands what is good, so that he will have something to share with one who has need. Let no unwholesome word proceed from your mouth, but only such a word as is good for edification according to the need of the moment, so that it will give grace to those who hear. Do not grieve the Holy Spirit of God, by whom you were sealed for the day of redemption. Let all bitterness and wrath and anger and clamor and slander be put away from you, along with all malice. Be kind to one another, tenderhearted, forgiving each other, just as God in Christ also has forgiven you. (Ephesians 4:25-32, NASB)

The Apostle says that unexpressed or bottled up anger gives the devil an opportunity in our lives, grieving the Holy Spirit, and giving bitterness, wrath, anger, clamor, slander, and malice a foothold. In verse 29 the word *unwholesome* means *rotten*. Anger can lead to rottenness if we allow it to just fester. It eventually will consume all that we do and all that we are. The end product of such stuffed anger becomes bitterness and unforgiveness.

To be human means occasional anger, but haven't we all known people for whom bitterness has become more than a passing phase? We can think of bitterness as the ossified form of anger. When we don't deal with our anger it gradually petrifies. If we continue to bury our anger, we risk becoming like a person dragging around the skeleton of a long-dead dinosaur. Unforgiveness weighs down our lives. It saps our strength and poisons our character.

Implosive anger has to find expression somehow so it results in passive-aggressive behavior, displaced anger, physiological and emotional stress, resentment, bitterness, and hatred. Imploders typically keep score; so living with one always carries the potential for a delayed explosion from a dormant volcano.

When Paul advised, "Do not let the sun go down on your anger," he wasn't dealing in religious platitudes. He was warning us to deal with our anger promptly and effectively before it spreads and does more damage. He also warned, "Do not give the devil an opportunity." Paul explained the poorly managed anger offers the devil a *topos* —the Greek word from which we get *topography*. It means a plot of land.

Imagine that you are fighting a war—because you are by the way. The very last thing you would want would be to freely grant your enemy a military base from which to launch more attacks into your life and relationships. When you put anger in your refrigerator and save it for tomorrow, you grant your enemy that forward operating base. He will prove more than willing to lob mortar shells at you from the location you've allowed.

Implosive anger takes an emotion God built into each of us and makes it a self-destructive internal source of conflict. It may pop up at any time and always in the most unhealthy ways. Interestingly enough, we can practice both implosive anger and the opposite as well. Sometimes we toggle back and forth from imploding to exploding.

Explosive anger is the other unhealthy, ungodly management technique. We may manifest it as uncontrolled fury in a verbal and/or physical form. According to Ephesians 4:31 the outcome of all poorly managed anger is bitterness, wrath, more anger, clamor, slander, and malice.

Explosive anger verbally attacks by screaming, cursing, condemning, name-calling, humiliating, or threatening. It damages the self-esteem of both the giver and the recipient. Ultimately it destroys relationships because the exploder causes the anger recipient to retreat for emotional safety. Exploders frequently blame their victims for "making them mad," or they minimize their outbursts by labeling them "blowing off steam." In extreme cases the exploder may grab, push, or strike in anger. All unhealthy anger is harmful, but physical abuse should not be tolerated.

Toward a Healthy Alternative

Like water in a leaky container, unresolved anger never remains confined. It always finds some unhealthy way to express itself. Gary Chapman, author of *The Five Languages of Apology* says, "When one's sense of right is violated, that person will experience anger. He or she will feel wronged and resentful at the person (or persons) who have violated".

Abortion often causes us to react to things in ways we don't understand. They find themselves overreacting to events and circumstances in ways they don't expect-sometimes with anger, or other times with great sadness or hurt. Now that you are on your healing journey, you can begin to make sense of these uncomfortable emotions.

Common circumstances often trigger anger in women who have had abortions. Baby showers, mothers with children, books about fetal development, doctor visits, certain smells or odors can be triggers. Literature related to abortion, pregnant women, hospital nurseries and birth events can all push our buttons. Videos and TV programs related to pregnancy and birth, specific sounds, and pro-life/pro-choice advertisements and commercials add to our inner turmoil. Every woman describes different responses to these triggers. A specific sound or odor may cause nausea. Baby showers may bring feelings of dread. Women may avoid friends or family members who have children. Other women may become avid about pro-life or even pro-choice arguments as a way to deal with their abortion decision.

As we come face-to-face with our abortion decision, we are reminded of people who were involved in that choice. As we reflect on these people and their influence, we're reminded of the confusion, pressure, and perhaps the feeling that we had no other choice. As a result, a woman may aim her post-abortion anger at many targets. You may not even feel anger towards these targets, but rather your anger comes across as feelings of responsibility.

Potential targets of your anger many include: those who withheld the truth about abortion, friends who presented abortion as the best choice, yourself for allowing the unplanned pregnancy, doctors and nurses, extended family members, teachers or school counselors, church or religious leaders, the father of the baby, parents, God, the abortion clinic, the baby, media, and even lawmakers.

Often, we hesitate to admit our anger toward others for fear of rejection. We find ourselves defending those we feel we should love. In order to heal, it's important to acknowledge anger and release it in a healthy way.

Ephesians Anger Checklist

Based on many women's experience and the Ephesians passage, we have assembled a checklist to help you in evaluating and dealing with anger issues. Consider your responses to these areas and questions.

1) Assess Your Primary Emotion: Does my anger stem from loss of control, hurt, or indignation about wrongs?

2) Take Off Your Mask: What has hurt you? Talk through your feelings (Ephesians 4:25-26).

3) Deal with Issues and Confront: Have you learned to communicate issues clearly and early? Be sure the goal is resolving issues, not getting back at people (Ephesians 4:28).

4) Don't Let Anger Fester and Rot: Do you have unresolved anger? Buried anger scribbles a written invitation to the enemy to exploit us in wounding others and ourselves (Ephesians 4:29).

5) God Cares Deeply About Your Anger: Ask yourself, *have I turned my anger over to God?* His heart aches when we allow rages, resentment, or bitterness to take root and grow (Ephesians 4:30).

6) Replace Anger with Forgiveness and Compassion: Have you received the forgiveness God offers? Have you extended that forgiveness to others? Because God has forgiven us so much; we need to be willing to forgive others (Ephesians 4:32).

Heart to Heart from Pat

I am certain you have figured out by now that I am a pretty transparent person. We have made lots of confessions on this journey together so far, one of my first ones to you was that I am not an overly athletic person, and that is true, however I am a person who deeply loves the outdoors and God's creation in nature. I love being outdoors. I love the crystal-clear Gulf beaches that are minutes from my doorstep, I love snow covered mountain peaks and I have loved since my childhood, hiking in the tree-covered Blue Ridge Mountains. I love the smell of the crisp morning air, the deep thick green of the trees and the cool rumbling of mountain streams that always appear to be flowing up the mountain to me. Since I am an amateur hiker, at best, I always obey the warning signs. If one says "stay on the path", I stay on the path. If it says, "falling rocks", I keep my head on alert and when they say, "do not feed the bears, I choose another path!!"

God has built some warning signs into our lives to protect us from taking or staying on the wrong paths in life and to help us to define certain boundaries. Anger is an emotion that God gave us that when used correctly has the right result but when used in the wrong way, leads to death. I recently read a book about the things that steal the joy that God desires for us. Anger was high at the top. We studied together, several examples of the truth in our Bible study this past week. In the case of abortion, there are many areas that should cause anger in women and in God's people in general. We should be angry that women are lied to by doctors and medical professionals trusted to protect human life. We should be angry that women are pressured to have abortions by employers and educational institutions and inconvenienced social agencies. We should be angry that teenage girls are drawn by bold marketing ads placed by abortionists in high school newspapers telling them "no one has to know". However, we have learned through our study that anger that does not lead to healthy responses and positive actions, only leads to our own self-destruction and increased pain and loss.

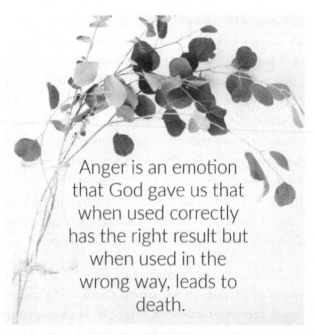

Anger is an emotion that God gave us that when used correctly has the right result but when used in the wrong way, leads to death.

For your Journal Time I am going to ask you to write some letters to some of the people who were involved in your abortion decision. It may have been a boyfriend, a parent or possibly one of those professionals that I mentioned before. **DON'T FORGET. THESE LETTERS ARE NOT TO BE MAILED!** I pray that just the writing of the letters helps you to understand how many people and circumstances actually played a part in your choice to abort. As alone as you may have felt walking into that abortion clinic, you were not alone in your decision. I pray that you have taken this opportunity to place some blame on other people beside yourself for a change, you have a right to do that. This exercise is meant to provide some safe boundaries and a safe place for you to identify and express your anger. Possibly, you have needed this time just to recognize that other people did play a part in your choice. You have been given some warning signs that will keep you on the right path so that your anger results in something positive, something that will make a difference for the Kingdom of God and something that will help heal your heart and release any strongholds that have been left in your life as a result of your abortion. Ephesians 4:26 says, "be angry, but sin not". Spend some time allowing God to show you the way to Freedom through those verses.

This process is going to be another one of those "weight loss" sessions. We are going to lighten our load a good bit at this point and from here on out you are going to begin to see a little bit more of the view. We are getting higher in our climb, as a matter of fact, after this session you will be halfway there! Take advantage of this time and this opportunity. It is safe, God planned it for you and it will help you get to your goal. I am continuing to pray for you

Chapter Four JOURNAL TIME

Spend some time reviewing the 6 Steps of the Ephesians anger check list mentioned in this chapter and write your response.

Write the steps adding your own name into the verses as appropriate. _____

_____

_____

_____

_____

_____

_____

_____

_____

Ask God to show you places of unidentified or unresolved anger from your past.

Take some time to write a letter to each person you have identified as someone you are or maybe SHOULD be angry with who was involved in you abortion experience.

After you are done, pray those words of scripture over those letters then take them somewhere safe and burn them or rip them to pieces as a symbol of surrendering them to God.

Close your time in prayer thanking God for the Freedom that is found in forgiveness.

JOURNAL TIME

_____

_____

_____

_____

_____

_____

_____

_____

_____

_____

_____

_____

_____

_____

_____

_____

_____

_____

_____

_____

_____

_____

_____

_____

God created all our
emotions for our
benefit—including
anger.

5

The Golden Key to Freedom

The process of working through anger can be exhausting. The next part of the journey to freedom from a past abortion is to release anger and lighten the load of this heavy burden you've been carrying. The goal of this chapter is to start moving from anger toward forgiveness.

As you begin to let go of your anger, think of it as healing you. Put the burden of resentment in God's hands. Recovery groups have long said that holding on to anger and un-forgiveness is like drinking poison and waiting for someone else to die from its effects. In the previous chapter, you took a look at the truth about abortion physically, spiritually and emotionally. To become angry is a normal response as we look at what the "free choice" for abortion is truly doing to our sisters, friends, daughters, and grandchildren.

As we saw in the last chapter, anger can be good. It can get things done. Anger can get our attention and result in action.

One caveat always applies to anger, however. The energy it generates must be channeled and directed. Untamed anger just lashes out at random. We must learn and discipline ourselves to guide its reactive energy to helpful ends. Then results can include change and restoration. Before we can express anger as a positive, we will look at the healing that comes from not only letting go of our damaging anger, but forgiving those who have hurt us.

In chapter four, we looked at the people involved in your abortion. Those people may include: the father of the child, nurses, doctors, parents, employers, school personnel, the pastor or church leaders, a counselor, and one or more friends. You may find yourself saying, "I want to stop being angry, but I just can't."

I'm afraid I must point you to an initially unwanted reality. If you want to experience true healing, at some point you have to make a decision to let go of your anger. The truth is, God wants us to go a step further: He wants us to forgive. In an area of our lives where we have been so hurt, it's difficult to imagine forgiving some of our offenders. However, with God's grace it is possible.

In referring to His people, God says, "I will forgive their wickedness and will remember their sins no more" (Jeremiah 31:34B, NIV). According to Jeremiah God forgives us completely. His example points us to a key element—what forgiveness does not entail. Before we can define what genuine forgiveness is and make a case for its necessity in healing, first we need to clarify what forgiveness is not.

Forgiveness is NOT forgetting. We frequently hear the phrase "forgive and forget," but forgiveness does not imply amnesia. When the Bible says that God "will remember their sins no more," it doesn't mean that He suddenly has no recollection of an offense. God does not develop a kind of heavenly Alzheimer's. It means that God chooses not to catalog our sins and use the information against us. God chooses to pass over His right to hold our wrongs against us.

Forgiveness is NOT minimizing the hurt. Forgiveness does not water down the offense by saying something like, "It's OK, it wasn't that bad." Or "I know that you didn't mean to hurt me." The truth is you've been hurt deeply and, sometimes, very intentionally. Forgiveness does not say, "I'm all right; it's just a flesh wound." When real trauma is involved. Instead, forgiveness calls the violation what is just as an umpire calls what he sees.

Forgiveness does NOT necessarily mean reconciliation. Perhaps you were thinking, "If I forgive the doctor, my ex-boyfriend, and my parents, then I have to initiate or at least be receptive to reconciliation." Hear this truth: forgiveness and reconciliation are two separate issues. Keep them apart. We definitely need to forgive for many reasons. We choose to reconcile or not to reconcile—and to what degree we reconcile—based on the facts of our situations.

Truthfully, some of you already are open to reconciliation and would give anything for it to happen, but reconciliation isn't even on the radar screen of some of the people involved in your abortion. Some people are unsafe for us and we most definitely should keep our distance from them. In some cases, the very thought of required reconciliation feels like being sentenced to life in prison without parole. Forgiveness recognizes that reconciliation may be neither possible nor wise following the abortion.

Relationships, and therefore reconciliation, are also matters of degree. Forgiving someone doesn't require becoming best friends or even close acquaintances with him or her. In some cases, you can genuinely forgive without ever initiating a relationship. In some cases, you may reconcile a relationship while maintaining your distance for any of a plethora of reasons. In some cases, you may find great love and support through reconciliation.

Some of these concepts or definitions may alter your view of forgiveness. You may find yourself more open to forgive those involved in your abortion when you dispense with wrong concepts of forgiveness.

The Bible tells a wonderful story about a young man who had every reason to hate and hold a grudge. He even had a delicious opportunity to experience the joy of a "pay back," but he chose a different response. Joseph's story begins in Genesis 37 and goes for ten chapters. You may want to take time to read it in its entirety before continuing to let God show you the way to redemptive healing.

Joseph was favored by his father but alienated from his brothers. When he was only seventeen, his brothers plotted to kill him but then tempered their actions by selling him into slavery. Thus he found himself a slave in the foreign kingdom of Egypt.

After years spent as a slave, Joseph was imprisoned for a crime he didn't commit. For thirteen years he faced shame and rejection. Through a series of divine interventions, Joseph left prison and became the second ruler of Egypt, reporting directly to Pharaoh. Ironically, he found himself facing the very brothers who wronged him, with them in great need of his help.

To add to the drama Joseph framed his brothers as thieves, and they did not recognize him. Joseph held in his hands the very thing for which bitter people everywhere long. He had all the power. Joseph could pay his brothers back. Unlimited revenge was within his grasp. His brothers didn't even know that Joseph could understand their language. With the brothers trembling in fear, Joseph... well, read the account directly from Genesis 45.

"Joseph could no longer keep his composure in front of all his attendants, so he called out, 'Send everyone away from me!' No one was with him when he revealed his identity to his brothers. But he wept so loudly that the Egyptians heard it, and also Pharaoh's household heard it. Joseph said to his brothers, 'I am Joseph! Is my father still living?' But his brothers were too terrified to answer him. Then Joseph said to his brothers, 'Please, come near me,' and they came near. 'I am Joseph, your brother,' he said, 'the one you sold into Egypt. And now don't be worried or angry with yourselves for selling me here, because God sent me ahead of you to preserve life. For the famine has been in the land these two years, and there will be five more years without plowing or harvesting. God sent me ahead of you to establish you as a remnant within the land and to keep you alive by a great deliverance. Therefore, it was not you who sent me here, but God. He has made me a father to Pharaoh, lord of his entire household, and ruler over all the land of Egypt.' " Genesis 45:1-8, HCSB

Joseph's brothers were terrified when they recognized him. They had sold him into slavery years before. They never imagined that he would be second in command in Egypt. For all they knew he was dead.

Joseph's perspective about God enabled him to forgive his brothers. He saw God's hand in everything that had happened. Being sold into slavery had resulted in his chance to save the lives of his father and his brothers.

Joseph had every reason and opportunity to repay his brothers for the agony they caused him. Joseph, however, did not choose to take that opportunity. He forgave them because he'd allowed love to replace bitterness and because he's learned the truth the apostle Paul later expressed in Romans 8:28. Joseph understood that "God causes all things to work together for good to those who love God, to those who are called according to His purpose" (Romans 8:28, NASB).

The New Testament of course further enforces the need to forgive. A man came to Jesus and asked how many times he had to forgive his brother. Matthew 18 records Jesus' response with a story. Jesus described a man who owed a vast amount of money. The holder of his debt decided to have the man and his entire family thrown in a debtor's prison, but the man begged for leniency. The master forgave the massive debt and the man promptly accosted another man who owed him a small debt. When the master heard what the forgiven debtor had done, he summoned him and said, "'you wicked slave! I forgave you all that debt because you begged me. Shouldn't you also have had mercy on your fellow slave as I had mercy on you?'" (Matt. 18:32-33).

As the consummate rabbi, Jesus knew the most powerful way

to teach is to lay out the truth but allow the hearers to make the connections for themselves. In the story of the debtor, the underlying question is how can we so petty as to refuse to forgive the relatively small debt of what others have done to us when God has forgiven us the massive wrong of our sin debt? If even the most sinned-against among us were pile up all the wrongs they have endured could the list ever compare to what the perfect and totally innocent Son of God endured?

God requires us to forgive anyone who offends us. He does not give us the option to choose whom we'll forgive and against whom we will continue to hold a grudge. Paul wrote: "Make allowance for each other's faults, and forgive anyone who offends you. Remember, the Lord forgave you, so you must forgive others" (Colossians 3:13 NLT).

God commands us to forgive for His glory, for the healing of others and for our own benefit. Forgiveness helps maintain harmony in relationships. It also creates deep peace and joy in the lives of the two captives it sets free- your offender and you!

As a woman who has faced the pain and loneliness of abortion, you have a reason to be angry with many people- at the very least the lawmakers, media, and medical community who have betrayed their responsibility to protect life and to ensure truth. You have reason to be angry and to feel cheated by some of your loved ones and your circumstances.

True forgiveness is seldom easy. It can be quite costly, but it offers us a powerful weapon for tearing down strongholds in our lives and hearts. The enemy uses unforgiveness and anger to keep us in bondage. When we surrender our unforgiveness and anger, we set our own hearts free so God can take us places we never dreamed possible.

Barriers to forgiveness

A number of barriers can hinder a person from letting go of anger and interfering in the healing process. A few examples include:

If I forgive the offender, he or she will never understand the severity of the act.

If I forgive, I will look weak; I have my pride.

He/she doesn't deserve forgiveness, only punishment. I can't let him/her off the hook.

Forgiveness isn't possible for this (I believe abortion is unforgivable).

The offender shows no remorse, so I have no responsibility to forgive.

If I let go of my anger, I may also let go of my child.

Letting go of anger means letting go of my relationships with persons involved in the abortion (sometimes anger is the only emotion connecting people).

I'm comfortable with the status quo, and I'm afraid of the unknowns that will come.

Benefits and Consequences

We often believe the lie that our anger effectively punishes the offender. The truth is that we are the only one undergoing punishment. We punish ourselves and are imprisoned by it.

Frederick Buechner writes in *Wishful Thinking:*

> *Of the Seven Deadly Sins, anger is possibly the most fun. To lick your wounds, to smack your lips over grievances long past, to roll over your tongues the prospect of bitter confrontations still to come, to savor to the last toothsome morsel both the pain you are given and the pain you are giving back- in many ways it is a feast fit for a king. The chief drawback is that what you are wolfing down is yourself. The skeleton at the feast is you. When we choose to forgive, we release our prisoner from the dungeon and discover that we are subsequently freed from the dank cell of our own bitterness. Spiritually and emotionally, forgiveness frees us.*

In Genesis 50:20, Joseph told his brothers, "You intended to harm me, but God intended it for good to accomplish what is now being done, the saving of many lives" (NIV). You may not even imagine being able to say these words.

Forgiving Yourself

Many people in our culture talk about forgiving ourselves. We post-abortive women commonly feel that while God has forgiven us, we cannot seem to forgive ourselves. We need to grasp a crucial truth that may surprise many. God never intended for us to forgive ourselves. The Bible does not identify the need to forgive ourselves. In fact, I don't think we are capable of it.

The key is not forgiving yourself but accepting God's forgiveness. When we try to forgive ourselves, we seek to do God's work in His place. The distinction may trouble you and seem like semantics, but it goes to the very heart of the Scripture and the Gospel. Let me try to explain with two biblical examples.

In the Garden of Eden God gave our first human parents a division of labor—not between Adam and Eve but between the pair and God. They were to take care of the tasks He gave them. Tend the garden; populate the earth, that sort of human stuff. God was to take care of the God stuff. But in Genesis 3 Satan came and tempted Eve with the thought that God was holding out on them. If they would just disobey God and make their own decisions (eat the fruit), they would become "like God, knowing good and evil."

For millennia theologians have debated and tried to describe the heart of Eve and Adam's sin. They use pride other terms, but this is certain. Eve wanted to have what God had and to take over his place.

What does that have to do with forgiving? You may ask. In the same way forgiving is God's territory, not ours. Only He is holy. All sin may hurt us, but it is ultimately against Him. Only He has the infinite power to forgive. When we push Him aside like a petulant preschooler and say "me do it," we only interfere with the process.

Allow me a second biblical illustration from the Gospel. The Gospel is the good news that Christ has died for our sins, to do for us what we could never do for ourselves. The Gospel means much more than simply forgiveness, but it certainly means no less. Ephesians 2 underscores the glorious fact that the Gospel is a gift. "For by grace you are saved through faith, and this is not from yourselves; it is God's gift— not from works, so that no one can boast" (Ephesians 2:8-9, HCSB).

What would happen if someone were to say, "I would rather do it myself? I don't have to rely on the gift (though it cost the Son of God's death). I choose to do it myself." The question is not hypothetical, for every day people reject the Gospel and choose to "do it themselves." In the words of Dr. Phil, "How's that working out?"

Please don't miss this application in either of two ways. First don't miss the giant cosmic application. If you have been trying to justify yourself, even the tiniest bit, stop it! Recognize that you cannot be good enough for God. Stop trying to make yourself pleasing and accept the reality that Christ presents us as a perfect offering to God. As a friend says, "If Jesus death on the cross didn't make God happy (big theological word: propitiation), nothing you do is going to make Him happy.

Then don't miss the smaller but critically important application: you can't forgive you. That's God's job. His forgiveness is a gift. Accept it.

Now having said that, we need to come back and say that accepting forgiveness for yourself and living with the reality that you are forgiven is absolutely essential. You don't need to be forgiven over and over for the same sin. You do, however, need to dip yourself again and again in the reality that if you are in Christ, you are a new creation.

Heart to Heart from Pat

Many years ago, I found myself at a place in life that was not what every little girl dreams of. I was wallowing in the ugly results of lots of bad choices. My marriage was falling apart; my two young sons were living in a very bad family environment that was going nowhere and fast. My life was falling apart and I had no idea how to fix it. I had actually spent several years and several thousand dollars with a secular therapist who told me to dump my husband and my kids and find myself. Thank the Lord that I had enough of Him in me from my childhood that I knew that was not my answer. Since I didn't know what else to do, I went to church. I was deeply in shame and guilt and so afraid of anyone finding out who I really was, but at the same time desperate for a change in my life. After a few months of hiding out in the Sunday School rooms with my two sons because I was too afraid to go to "big church" a beautiful young woman named Terri invited me to come with her to a weekend ladies retreat. The topic of the retreat, I was to later discover, was anger. I was not aware of any "anger" in my life, lots of bad things but not anger, or so I thought. I agreed to go with her and that was the day that I surrendered my life to Christ. I turned my heart over to Him-fully, completely and passionately. When I rushed to the alter that day at the speakers invitation, my life was a mess. I had nothing to offer the Lord but my broken heart. It was many, many years later before that message on anger really sunk in for me. I pray that over the past few chapters, you have grasped a better understanding of the many ways unresolved anger can show up in our lives and become a stronghold for the enemy to keep us trapped in, without our even knowing it. During your Journal Time you will be given an opportunity to decide and declare that anger and unforgiveness will hold you back no longer.

So far on this journey we have had some heavy loads to carry, thirst to overcome, and it has felt like a few mountain lions to slay! It is time we to clear some paths so that we can get a peek at the view. We have talked about my family backpack as a visual reminder of the burden caused by carrying unhealthy and ungodly behaviors and emotions on our journey with God. We have lightened it a bit each week with the junk that God wants us to dump off and leave behind — secrets, lies and anger. In the amplified bible, Hebrews 12:1 says we are instructed to strip off, throw aside every unnecessary weight, and the sin that clings to us and entangles us. Can't you just picture that entanglement in your life? It says that we are to press on with patient endurance, steady and persistent, the race, or the journey, that God has planned for us.

Mark 11:25 says, "whenever you are praying, if you have anything against anyone, forgive him and let it drop, leave it, let it go in order that your Father in Heaven may also forgive you your own failings and short coming and let them drop" (amp)

I cannot speak for you but I for certain want my failings and short coming to be dropped by those who have charges against me. Early in my own walk with God, I began to change my focus from the failures and abuse that I had received from others, to look upon my own sin and failure. It is such a difficult process but always clears the path for us to walk straight into the arms of our Lord.

In this chapter we have learned about getting some things out of our way that have been blocking our walk with the Lord. We have looked in our study at what forgiveness is and what it is not. True forgiveness is not a feeling but rather it is a choice, this time a choice for life and not death.

Forgiveness is an act of obedience to God and an act of surrender that will allow His full blessing on your life as you release the entanglement of holding onto unforgiveness. When we forgive a person, he or she is permanently forgiven. When Satan tries to drag you back down and make you think that you haven't really forgiven someone, you just speak right back at him the words of truth that you have captures this week. We are to forgive the same way that God forgives, supernaturally, permanently, and unconditionally. This is going to be an amazing session, one that I truly feel you will never forget.

In my home, I have a special place where I meet God. It is a big fluffy, overstuffed green chair in my living room. It has been reupholstered many times. I call it my prayer chair. I have a basket next to my chair with my reading glasses, a few different bibles, my journal and some pens and highlighters. I have whatever bible study I am currently working on and I have a few prayer books like *Praying God's Word* by Beth Moore and one called *Prayers that Avail Much*.

As you step out into this life changing work of forgiveness, I would like to pray for you again, a prayer that I myself have prayed many times from the pages of that little book.

When I have been faced with a person or situation that calls for me to release anger and seek what God has for me to hear and learn.

Father, in the name of Jesus, we make fresh commitment to you to live in peace and harmony, not only with brothers and sisters in the body of Christ but also with our friends, associates, neighbors and family and yes Lord, even our enemies. We let go of all bitterness, resentment, envy, strife and unkindness in any form. We give no place to the devil in Jesus' name. Now Father, my sisters and I ask your forgiveness. By faith, we receive it, having assurance that we are cleansed from all unrighteousness through Jesus Christ. We ask you to forgive and release all who have wronged and hurt us. Together, we forgive and release them. Deal with them in your mercy Lord, and loving-kindness, as we would have you deal with us. From this moment on, we purpose to walk in love, to seek peace, to live in agreement and to conduct ourselves in a manner that is pleasing to you. We know that we have right standing with you Lord and that you are attentive to our prayers. It is written in your word that your love has been poured into our hearts by your Holy Spirit. We desire to be filled with your righteousness which brings glory and honor to you.

Amen, so be it!

Chapter Five JOURNAL TIME

Let me suggest you write Scripture on cards to read and memorize. Here are just some suggestions, but know that the Bible is absolutely full of affirmations of God's forgiveness. That's what the Gospel is all about.

"He has rescued us from the domain of darkness and transferred us into the kingdom of the Son He loves, 14 in whom we have redemption, the forgiveness of sins." (Colossians 1:13-14, HCSB)

"In him we have redemption through his blood, the forgiveness of sins, in accordance with the riches of God's grace" (Ephesians 1:7, NIV).

"If we confess our sins, [God] is faithful and righteous to forgive us our sins and to cleanse us from all unrighteousness" (1 John 1:9, HCSB).

God is the One who saves us, forgives us, and redeems us. Forgiving ourselves does not achieve forgiveness from sin. According to both passages in Ephesians we cannot do anything to earn forgiveness, rather it is a gift of God's grace. Only God can forgive our sins against Him, but we have to confess them. That is the only requirement, confession.

When we as Christ-followers say, "I know God can forgive me, but I can't forgive myself," we are elevating our ability to forgive and seeking to take on ourselves God's ability. True healing and freedom only occur when we can accept the forgiveness God so graciously wants to give each of us. In not completely accepting God's forgiveness, you're essentially buying the lies that Christ's sacrifice on the cross was not sufficient to cover your abortion.

How sweet the reality that if we confess our sins, wounds, failures, and false beliefs to God, He'll forgive, renew, transform, restore, and redeem us.

I have prayed for you. Now take some time to write your own prayer.

_____

_____

_____

_____

_____

_____

_____

_____

_____

_____

_____

_____

_____

_____

_____

_____

_____

Forgiveness is NOT forgetting.
Forgiveness is NOT minimizing the hurt.
Forgiveness does NOT necessarily mean reconciliation.

6

The Great Exchange

Tears welled up from the depths of my soul. I felt as if they'd never stop. That night of sobbing in the bathtub was a major turning point for me. The truth of what I had done to my child had finally sunk into my heart, and the grief overwhelmed me. Abortion had taken so much from me! I grieved over my sinful choices, the struggles in my life, my wounded heart, and, most of all, my precious baby.

After thirty-three years of carrying the burden myself, I finally gave my sin to God. I thought I'd already done that at the ladies' retreat, but I'd stopped short. Abortion was the last thing on my mind that day at the altar. So much more had happened afterwards. What I had given to God there was my broken life—my marriage, my emotions, my needs, and my expectations. I gave what I knew to give. The night in the bathtub, however, I faced the cross. For the first time, I understood the sin that Jesus had personally carried to the cross for me. I understood the darkness of my heart at a level far beyond my personal needs. I understood that I could not save myself, that I needed a rescuer. Not until that night did I grasp the amazing depth of my Rescuer's love for me.

As I cried, I washed as though I could wash away all the dirt and pain of my life. In truth, I scrubbed at my body the way a rape victim tries to wash away the violent invasion of rape. As I bathed, I grasped the meaning of the cross at a deeper level and gratefully accepted the sacrifice of the cross. I understood that Jesus Christ willingly gave His life for mine— to set me free, to heal me, and to redeem my entire life.

Gradually, the tears for my own loss transformed into tears for the incredible burden that Jesus took on Himself and the passionate love that drove Him to shoulder it. My burden was more than I could bear, but He bore the burden of every person on the planet.

While I began the night releasing tears, I ended it by releasing my grip on my sins, my hurts, and my burdens. A year earlier at the ladies' retreat, I surrendered my head. That night in the bathtub, I surrendered my heart.

The cleansing I felt was amazing! It was wonderful! It still is.

In the last chapter we made great progress in our journey toward forgiving those involved in our abortions. We also began to understand and accept god's forgiveness for us. The path of forgiveness is intertwined with the path of grieving. As our losses from abortion become more real to us, we will grieve more deeply and, in that grief, we'll need to revisit the step of forgiveness. As we move together to step 6 on our map, we'll focus on the importance of grieving our losses and receiving God's gift of wholeness.

Two Kinds of Sorrow

Any traumatic event in our lives will create sorrow. Many people experience deep sorrow that leads to depression, addictions, and a host of other dark places of the soul.

Grieving does not however have to be destructive. God gave us the gift of grieving as a way to deal with life's difficulties and disappointments. The apostle Paul explained the difference between two kinds of sorrow in his second letter to the Corinthian church. He actually said he was glad the Corinthians were experiencing sorrow.

Now I'm glad—not that you were upset, but that you were jarred into turning things around. You let the distress bring you to God, not drive you from him. The result was all gain, no loss. Distress that drives us to God ... turns us around. It gets us back in the way of salvation. We never regret that kind of pain. But those who let distress drive them away from God are full of regrets, and end up on a deathbed of regrets. And now, isn't it wonderful all the ways in which this distress has goaded you closer to God? You're more alive, more concerned, more sensitive, more reverent, more human, more passionate, more responsible. Looked at from this angle, you've come out of this with purity of heart. (2 Corinthians 7:9-11, The Message)

Paul differentiates between godly distress/sorrow and destructive distress/sorrow. Godly sorrow causes someone to turn back to God. It leads to repentance and never causes regret. On the other hand, destructive sorrow drives people away from God and does cause regret.

In past chapters, we discovered the importance of replacing lies—false beliefs we've embraced—with truth from God. If we'll allow our pain and sorrow to drive us toward God rather than away from Him, we'll experience transformation, healing, and new life.

Because past memories, sorrow, and hurts are uncomfortable for us, we try to avoid them or find ways to escape the pain. And yet, Paul was happy about the Corinthians' struggles and distress because it jarred them into change. Jesus also promoted godly sorrow and gave those who are hurting a wonderful promise:

"Blessed are those who mourn, because they will be comforted." (Matthew 5:4, HCSB)

Jesus promises comfort to those who mourn. Remembering and grieving our losses are vital in the healing process. It allows us to remember where we have come from and how God worked in those circumstances.

Our Trustworthy Guide

As we're truly open about our feelings with God, he'll take us further down the path to healing. Most of us, though, have doubts about God's goodness and, specifically, about his heart toward us personally. Let's see what God says about us.

"Do not be afraid, for I have ransomed you. I have called you by name; you are mine. When you go through deep waters, I will be with you. When you go through rivers of difficulty, you will not drown. When you walk through the fire of oppression, you will not be burned up; the flames will not consume you. For I am the Lord, your God, the Holy One of Israel, your Savior." (Isaiah 43:1b-3a, NLT)

"On that day you will not be put to shame for all the wrongs you have done to me, because I will remove from this city those who rejoice in their pride. Never again will you be haughty on my holy hill. But I will leave within you the meek and humble, who trust in the name of the Lord... The Lord has taken away your punishment; he has turned back your enemy. The Lord, the King of Israel, is with you; never again will you fear any harm. ... The Lord your God is with you, he is mighty to save. He will take great delight in you, he will quiet you with his love, he will rejoice over you with singing." (Zephaniah 3:11-12,15,17, NIV)

God gave Isaiah several assurances when he faced various fears. He promised to be with Isaiah. Difficulties would not drown him; oppression would not burn him nor would the flames of oppression consume him.

God promised that he won't put his children to shame (Zeph. 3:11) and will take away our punishment (Zeph. 3:15). However, God does require us to embrace some vital heart attitudes. He wants us to be meek, humble, and trusting.

Zephaniah 3:17 says that God takes delight in us and rejoices over us. Doesn't that provide you such comfort?

Fear is often the greatest enemy to meaningful life change. We long to return to what's familiar rather than take risks and face the unknown. More than anything else, the healing journey requires that we trust God. Healing the wounds in our innermost being will lead us down paths we never could have imagined. So, we take one day and one step at a time as we walk into the shadows with Jesus. We allow him to turn the shadows to light, to ease our pain, and to lead us into freedom, truth, and the desires of our hearts.

We have focused on the vital step of grieving our losses. The next step in our journey will open our minds and hearts to the incredible vistas that await us at the summit of our climb. We can become more than we've been and more than we realize. It's time to make the great exchange—to accept who we really are in Christ.

"Blessed are those who mourn, because they will be comforted."

Matthew 5:4, HCSB

Change from the Inside Out

God's forgiveness, which comes with our confession, is a very powerful force in our lives. God's blessings don't stop when we receive salvation. He wants to help us really change. That happens through our repentance. Unfortunately, that word has been given a bad connotation over the years. Repent comes from the Greek word *metanoia*, which means to change (*meta*) our mind or understanding (*noia*).   The word metamorphosis is a related term, meaning a change in form or substance, and is used to describe what occurs when a caterpillar retreats into its cocoon to emerge as a butterfly. This is a wondrous thing, but God does even more wondrous things for his children.

"Pay attention, O Jacob, for you are my servant, O Israel. I, the Lord, made you, and I will not forget you. I have swept away your sins like a cloud. I have scattered your offenses like the morning mist. Oh, return to me, for I have paid the price to set you free." Sing, O heavens, for the Lord has done this wondrous thing. Shout for joy, O depths of the earth! Break into song, O mountains and forests and every tree! For the Lord has redeemed Jacob and is glorified in Israel." (Isaiah 44:21-23, NLT)

God's words in Isaiah 44 apply to the history of Israel, but they also give us an excellent starting place for our repentance. According to verses 21-22, God not only will not forget each one of us, but He sweeps away our sins. He scatters them like the mist and has paid the price of our freedom.

Romans 12:1-2 and John 8:31-32 clarify further by separating the process of repentance or transformation into God's part and our part.

"I urge you, brothers, in view of God's mercy, to offer your bodies as living sacrifices, holy and pleasing to God —this is your spiritual act of worship. Do not conform any longer to the pattern of this world, but be transformed by the renewing of your mind. Then you will be able to test and approve what God's will is —His good, pleasing, and perfect will." (Romans 12:1-2, NIV)

"Jesus said...'If you continue in My word, you really are My disciples. 32 You will know the truth, and the truth will set you free.'" (John 8:31-32, HCSB)

God doesn't expect you to change your own life. He asks that you make yourself available to His Holy Spirit by remaining in His presence. As we turn to God and begin to give him our secrets, our shame, false beliefs, and distorted perspectives, we become engaged in a battle of the mind and heart. Recall the model we discussed in chapter two in which our wounds become infected with lies that lead to destructive agreements and a false sense of self.

"For though we live in the world, we do not wage war as the world does. The weapons we fight with are not the weapons of the world. On the contrary, they have divine power to demolish strongholds. We demolish arguments and every pretension that sets itself up against the knowledge of God, and we take captive every thought to make it obedient to Christ." (2 Corinthians 10:3-5, NIV)

The cosmic battle between good and evil is not waged on Earth. It occurs in a realm that we cannot see or even really understand. We must demolish the "strongholds" that set themselves up against God.

Today we don't use the word *stronghold* very often today. Imagine castles, fortresses, or even a battle scene from a movie like Braveheart or Lord of the Rings. Strongholds are enemy fortresses in our territory made of lies we have allowed to take root in our lives. Anything that is contrary to God and His Word can become an enemy foothold.

Destroying these fortresses of falsehood takes a lot of time, muscle, and energy. In my life I imagine massive armies attacking and weapons such as cannons and explosives crumbling these structures to the ground.

As we recognize the battle being waged over our minds and hearts, we begin to understand why change must occur from the inside out. God must do the work in our innermost being—our hearts and minds. He transforms us. Our part in repentance is to persistently decide to turn or return to God.

Grieving Our Losses

God sees your pain, your losses, and shame. He not only gives you permission to grieve your losses, but He invites you to grieve. Grief is the process God created to help us deal with the inevitable losses of life. As you come to grips with what abortion has taken away from you, then you can leave it at Jesus' feet "where grace and mercy meet."

God doesn't expect you
to change your own life.
He asks that you make
yourself available to His
Holy Spirit by remaining
in His presence.

God longs to comfort you and to set you free so you can lift your head.

While it may be painful, it is important to acknowledge the losses—those things, opportunities, people, relationships, experiences, or feelings that abortion either has taken away from you or never allowed you to experience. If you are one who journals or has been keeping a journal during the time you have been reading this book, I want to encourage you to write about the things God brings to your mind.

Now close your eyes and imagine Jesus walking into the room, putting His arms around you, and gently speaking these words to you:

"Do not be afraid, for I have ransomed you. I have called

you by name; you are mine. When you go through deep waters, I will be with you. When you go through rivers of difficulty, you will not drown. When you walk through the fire of oppression, you will not be burned up; the flames will not consume you. For I am the Lord, your God, the Holy One of Israel, your Savior." (Isaiah 43:1b-3a, NLT)

At this point in your journey, it's important to understand what happened with Jesus at the cross. True and lasting freedom only comes as we understand the ransom price Jesus paid for our freedom, and as we accept His payment as our only hope of salvation and real life. If you have questions about accepting Jesus' sacrifice and free gift of eternal salvation, please ask your pastor, Christian friend, or another committed Christian that you know.

Steps to the Cross

1) God created you and loves you. (Genesis 1:26-27; John 3:16-18)

2) We've fallen from our original glory. (Genesis 3:1,13; Romans 3:23)

3) Jesus came to rescue you from darkness and captivity. (Colossians 1:12-14)

4) Jesus is your only hope for abundant and eternal life. (John 14:6)

5) You must choose life (John 1:12-13; John 5:24)

All Things New

Too often we see ourselves as the sum of all our failures. We get blinded to who we really are and how God sees us after we've placed our trust in Jesus to rescue and redeem us. According to 2 Corinthians 5:17-18, if anyone is in Christ, he or she becomes a "new creation". This means that when you come to accept Christ as your Lord and Savior you become new. Your old desires, your old inclinations, and your old nature have been replaced with Godly desires and a nature that He has given you. According to the verses from Ezekiel, God has given us His Spirit, which causes us to want to follow His way.

"Therefore, if anyone is in Christ, he is a new creation; the old has gone, the new has come! All this is from God, who reconciled us to himself through Christ and gave us the ministry of reconciliation." (2 Corinthians 5:17-18, NIV)

The Old Testament prophet Ezekiel provided us a beautiful picture of the new life Christ provides for us.

"I will sprinkle clean water on you, and you will be clean; I will cleanse you from all your filthiness and from all your idols. Moreover, I will give you a new heart and put a new spirit within you; and will remove the heart of stone from your flesh and give you a heart of flesh. I will put my Spirit within you and cause you to walk in My statutes, and you will be careful to follow My ordinances...you will be My people, and I will be your God." (Ezekiel 36:25-28, NASB)

Amazingly, God makes us entirely new creations when we place our faith in Jesus. For several reasons most of us never experience much of the new creation intends for us because:

- The enemy continues to deceive us, telling us God doesn't care and that we're nothing.
- We continue to live out of the well-worn patterns and ruts in our lives and don't embrace our new hearts and new lives.
- We block the work of the Holy Spirit by resisting Him or turning away from God, going our own way, and seeking satisfaction apart from Him.

God has so much more for you and me. He has places us in a favored position in His family, and we can step up to occupy that status as favored daughter

Your Favored Position on in God's Family

God's love is lavished on those who place their faith in Jesus. Because of nothing other than God's extreme love for us, we've been given a position that few of us have grasped, and even fewer live in. Our enemy clearly wants to keep this hidden, but Scripture clearly tells us we "did not receive a spirit of slavery to fall back into fear, but you received the Spirit of adoption, by whom we cry out, " Abba, Father!" The Spirit Himself testifies together with our spirit that we are God's children" (Romans 8:15-16, HCSB).

When we become children of God, we receive some amazing privileges. We are God's sons or daughters. We have literally been adopted into His family, but we also become heirs, which means we have an inheritance.

We've already been granted the privilege of the firstborn, but our position, as royalty won't be fully revealed until Jesus returns in His glory. "When Christ, who is our life, is revealed, then you also will be revealed with Him in glory" (Colossians 3:4, NASB). We participate spiritually in His death, resurrection, and glorification. We're daughters of the King of kings, co-heirs with Christ!

God wants this favored status to affect the way we approach life, the enemy, and enslavement to past sins and failures. Romans 8:15 plainly says that we have received a spirit of adoption and not of slavery or fear. That should give us some boldness sisters!

Trading Sorrows for Joy

The Bible is full of prophecies and promises that God will fulfill in part now and to the fullest extent when Jesus comes to take us into His eternal kingdom. Jeremiah 31 gives us one of these exciting prophecies for Israel, which also applies to Christ-follower under the New Covenant. Look at the passage and think how it fits both now and later.

They will come home and sing songs of joy on the heights of Jerusalem. They will be radiant because of the LORD's good gifts---the abundant crops of grain, new wine, and olive oil, and the healthy flocks and herds. Their life will be like a watered garden, and all their sorrows will be gone. The young women will dance for joy, and the men—old and young—will join in the celebration. I will turn their mourning into joy. I will comfort them and exchange their sorrow for rejoicing. The priests will enjoy abundance, and my people will feast on my good gifts. I, the LORD, have spoken!" (Jeremiah 13:12-14, NLT)

Although our current lives will still have troubles, God has given us His comfort which should cause us to rejoice greatly. Read verse 13 again, God will turn our mourning into joy and our sorrow into rejoicing. Yes, even our sorrow. Trust me, but more importantly trust Him.

If you have taken the steps to Surrender to Jesus for the first time or even RE-Surrender, record it here and write out each of the 5 steps with YOUR NAME in them!

_____

_____

_____

_____

_____

_____

_____

_____

_____

_____

_____

_____

_____

_____

_____

_____

_____

_____

Heart to Heart from Pat

We have come so very far on our journey, haven't we? God has helped you to confront possibly the darkest secret of your life, He has led you to truth about abortion that was hard but critical to hear, difficult to learn but has truly equipped you in a whole new way. You have faced some painful memories, confronted some long-hidden horrors and drawn out emotions that you never even knew existed. You have confronted some unhealthy anger that has been hindering, literally blocking your relationship with God. We have had a chance to blame everyone else for our abortion choice, for our bad care, for our unfair treatment, for our abandonment. But then, there comes that moment, when all else is moved aside and there is nothing left but you and God and your precious son or daughter.

I know that you have experienced many levels of the ultimate loss of your child, a loss that as women who have chosen abortion, we know to be a result of our own hand. We have destroyed our own innocent children, our own flesh and blood-bone of our bone and flesh of our flesh. In her book "The Desires of a Woman's Heart" Beverly LaHaye refers to the words of a popular Hollywood actress who positioned herself as a proponent of a woman's right to abortion, one of her very public speeches proclaimed that despite the fact that abortion is the killing of an innocent, defenseless life, and that it hurts women emotionally, physically and spiritually, claimed "it is my body, it is my nine months". Indeed, it was our body wasn't it sisters? It was our nine months. We are at a place in our journey, the point where we have nowhere to look but at ourselves as the ultimate one responsible for our children's death. The very good news is, we do not stop there, in our own grief and loss. We have learned more than that now, we have learned that our Lord has paid the price for our sin, His blood was shed to cover our shame, He has rescued us from the results of our own sin.

This is the time in the journey for an exchange to take place. The grief that we feel over the loss of our children is right and good, it does not have to be destructive and crippling. We have looked at the wonderful teaching that Paul left with us from 2 Corinthians 7:9-11 teaching us that our distress, our sorrow is to be used to draw us closer to our Lord. We have learned so far in our journey, how to replace lies or false beliefs for truth. It is time for us to allow our sorrow to drive us into the arms of our savior and to exchange our sin for His Holiness. We are about to move to new heights, no more weights to dump, no more brush to clear, now is the time to get refreshed and renewed.

Last year my sweet husband gave me a beautiful necklace as a gift for our anniversary. It has a diamond clasp and was such a precious and extravagant gift that I absolutely loved it; in our thirty plus years of marriage, it was one of my favorites of all gifts. Somehow, somewhere, one day, I discovered it was missing. I searched everywhere that I could think of and the necklace was nowhere to be found. I was devastated and heartbroken. Not only had he paid a sacrificial amount of money for it but I felt so sad to have lost such a heartfelt treasure. Months passed and I thought of that necklace so very often, feeling so ashamed of my carelessness. The following Christmas, my dear husband handed me a beautifully wrapped box and tucked inside was a new necklace, just like the one I had lost. That dear man had gone out and re-bought an identical new necklace for me to replace my own carelessly lost one.

The scripture that we have studied in Isaiah this past chapter has become one of my very favorite and most often claimed passages in God's word.

Every time I read its proclamation, I am recharged in the power of God's goodness and my position in His family. Ladies, we are daughters of the King of Kings. It is so time for us to take our places, to let the women of the world know who our Father is and what He has to say about abortion. It is so time for our voices to be the ones making change and establishing laws. It is time for us to take back what belongs to us! To speak Gods' word and truth on behalf of our daughters and friends. It is past time for our voices to be heard.

Let this session wash over you with its passion, cool you with its promise and cleanse your deepest loss with its peace. It is a gift to you from your Abba Father, a priceless gift that can never be lost.

Chapter Six JOURNAL TIME

Take some time after reading this chapter to write out, and more importantly remember, the day of your salvation.

When/Where did you SURRENDER YOUR LIFE to Jesus Christ? _____

_____

Re-read Isaiah 43:1-3 and express your feelings to God about being "ransomed" and called by name.

Express in your journal what your heart is feeling about God's amazing grace and unconditional love for you and for those involved in the heartbreak of abortion.

Spend some time thanking and praising God for all He has shown you so far in this study and begin to ask Him for HIS plan for your next step in the journey.

_____

_____

_____

_____

_____

_____

_____

_____

_____

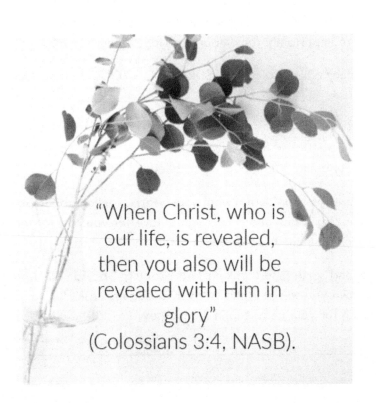

"When Christ, who is
our life, is revealed,
then you also will be
revealed with Him in
glory"
(Colossians 3:4, NASB).

7

The Peace of Release

I have always been an avid reader and writer. I've kept a daily prayer journal for more than thirty years, chronicling my healing journey and pouring out my emotions. Under my bed, I keep a stash of yellowing, spiral-bound notebooks. They share my story — one of a broken woman rescued by a mighty God. They're so personal — full of testimonies to God's grace, but also selfishness and silliness and whining — that I don't know what I want to do with them when I go home to Him.

But it was with the beginnings of those books that I took my first looks into God's Word. Apart from the ambiguities of the world, God's Word answered my questions clearly. I remember when God showed me Psalms 139:13-16 (NLT):

"You made all the delicate, inner parts of my body and knit me together in my mother's womb. Thank you for making me so

wonderfully complex! Your workmanship is marvelous — how well I know it. You watched me as I was being formed in utter seclusion, as I was woven together in the dark of the womb.

You saw me before I was born. Every day of my life was recorded in your book. Every moment was laid out before a single day had passed."

As I envisioned my aborted child, my heart dropped. My grief encompassed me. As I learned how God felt about my baby — about every baby — I experienced fresh pain. I cried. I collapsed to the bedroom floor and buried my head in my arms. I cried out, this time to God, in sorrow and in the solitude of my significant loss. Tears welled up from the depths of my soul, and it felt as if they'd never stop.

It was then that the Lord gave me a vision, of a little girl in a frilly pink dress. She was beautiful with long blonde hair and short arms outstretched to me. She smiled and then said, "It's OK, Mommy. I am happy here with Jesus. I forgive you and love you. I'll be here waiting when you come, but Jesus has some things for you to do first."

Little did I know all that He had in mind for my complete healing and restoration.

He has the same dream for you!

He has...

More than You can Hope or Imagine

Surreal is the best word to describe my feelings as I walked down the long, white hospital corridor leading into the Neonatal Intensive Care Unit of Tampa's largest Woman's hospital. The space was filled with white walls, white ceilings, and bare windows. An emotional battle raged in my heart and head. My husband and I walked the seemingly endless hallway together, just as we had so many years before. This day we were here to meet our soon-to-be baby daughter. Our hearts were drawn to meet her. My head was stuck in memories of another time when we had taken a similar walk, down a different corridor, in this same hospital. Twelve years before, we'd had an abortion here. It all seemed so bazaar. The circumstances of each event were amazing unto itself.

As Mike and I rounded the corner of the NICU into the open nursery area, we were both trembling, gripping hands so tightly as to cut off all feeling. The room was filled with babies. Most were inside of clear plastic boxes with two little "portholes" in the front for the doctors and nurses to slip their hands through when caring for the sick and tiny babies. Some babies lay naked with tiny arms and legs flailing wildly and all kinds of tubes and wires attached to them for monitoring of every body function. They lay on chest high podium-like tables covered with soft, white sheepskin.

That is how we first saw her. A tiny baby girl. TINY being the key word. The nurses had named her Julianna. Juli for the July month of her birth, and Anna for the prophetic beauty of the name. Julianna had been born to a seventeen-year-old girl at approximately twenty-three weeks gestation. Her birth weight was a whopping 1-1/2 pounds! She was 10" long. The day we met Julianna, she had recently undergone some surgery and had dropped to only one pound. She was barely the size of a matchbox! She was without question, the most incredible and beautiful thing I had ever seen. As I looked upon her face for the first time, doctors and nurses had gathered around to see for themselves the couple who had come upon the scene to adopt Julianna. They were very protective and concerned. I was in a trance. It took all that I had to contain my balance and not swoon to the floor as I heard the sweet voice of God speak to my heart, "This, Pat, is what I create in a mother's womb, this is why I have called you to do the work I have called you to do." I felt overwhelming surety that God had literally place a "pre-born" child in my presence.

As I looked upon Julianna, my mind was reeling that very reality, "the work" He had recently "called me to do." I was very certain that God had called me not many months before to open Tampa, Florida's first Crisis Pregnancy Center. As I stood beside that tiny baby lying in the center of that white, sheepskin table, a large group of my closest friends were hard at work back at my insurance agency, painting, wallpapering, and preparing some vacant space in the back half of my office to become a Crisis Pregnancy Center. I had "recruited" them to join up with the vision God had given me and they had eagerly responded. We were set to open in just a few more months. God was clearly leading the way. His favor preceded our every move. I was running my own insurance business out of the front office and preparing for ministry out of the back. Donations were coming from every direction; paint, wallpaper, office supplies, pregnancy test, furniture, on and on the blessings flowed.

From the moment I had asked Christ into my heart He moved into my life in a mighty way. He surrounded me with strong, Christian mentors who were committed to helping me learn as much as I could about God and His ways. They taught me to love the Word of God and to pray. They were relentless in their unconditional love as the many walls of my past and my pain had to be crumbled in my life as I was set on a whole new path. The Lord knew how important these friends would be to me as I struggled to believe that He could truly forgive a past as sinful as mine had been. I will never forget the day that He gently revealed the truth about abortion to me. My immediate temptation was to hide away and never tell my Christian friends. I was convinced that once they knew the horrible truth, they could not accept me anymore. Of course, I was very wrong. Not only did they accept and love me, they became the wind under my wings as they encouraged me into the plans God had for my life. What an awesome God He is, thinking through every detail!

As I stood amidst the flurry of activity within the NICU, my thoughts swirled over the events of the past few days...

My life was in a non-stop wave of activity as I daily ran a full-time insurance agency, parented two sons; an eighteen-year-old senior in High school, and a pre-teen ten-year-old. All the while, I was deeply involved in the excitement of preparing the way for the Crisis Pregnancy Center. It was deep in this time when my husband, Mike, woke up one morning and announced, "I think we should adopt a baby girl!" My response wasn't exactly overflowing with Proverbs 31 when I responded in my old Pat ways with, "are you crazy! Can't you see how busy my life is? Does it look like I have time for a baby? Besides, we have a senior!" Needless to say, I was shocked and a bit miffed.

We had discussed the possibility of adoption on several occasions. We had two sons and I had longed for a daughter for many years. I had always believed in my heart that my aborted child was a little girl. It has just never happened. Too expensive. Too much red tape. Where do you start? Time passed and it was only small talk. Until that day I told

Mike it was impossible. Bad timing. No way! Fortunately with God, NOTHING is impossible. His ways are not our ways!

With God, NOTHING is impossible.

Mike arrived home from work that same afternoon looking frazzled and pale. He had taken the liberty, as only a man would do, of inquiring of an attorney friend of ours that day at work about the possibilities of adopting a child, maybe a toddler. "Do you believe in divine intervention?" the friend asked Mike. "Absolutely...why?" Mike asked his friend. Our friend proceeded to tell Mike that He had just hung up the phone with the hospital and they had a little baby girl whose birth mother desired to place for adoption. Our friend knew that the sixty-something families he had on his list would probably be skeptical about this adoption. He proceeded to tell Mike, "this little girl was born three months early and she weighs only one pound. She is likely to have serious life-long health challenges. She will possibly be blind, unable to hear, and could be retarded. It is difficult to determine and probably will be for a long time. We are not even certain she will live." Mike relayed our morning conversation to our friend, promptly assuring him that I would probably not be interested, but he would talk to me that night.

We sat on our bedside as my husband relayed the remarkable story to me that evening. We were both overwhelmed with emotion. In typical "Pat" fashion, I got right to work. I decided to call everyone I knew who was interested in adopting a child. The first one I called was one of my very dear "God friends," Elaine. Elaine and I had become friends through a ministry we had founded together called, Sisters of Rachel, a healing ministry for women who have had abortions in their past. Elaine had an abortion in her late teens. That aborted child turned out to be the only child she would ever conceive. She was unable to become pregnant again and longed for a child. She was the first one I called. She listened intently to Julianna's story. Then she was very quiet on the other end of the telephone. "What do you think, Elaine?" I asked her. "I think I would absolutely love to have that little girl, but I can't," she replied.

"Why not, Elaine? God will work this out. He can bring this child through. I know He can" I told her. "Oh, I am certain that He will bring her through, Pat, but this baby is not for me...God planned this little girl for you and Mike!"

I can remember the chair I was sitting in, the level of the sun outside the window, the clarity of the blue sky, and the tears that rolled down my cheeks. She IS for me. That little tiny girl that I have never seen is going to be my daughter. Mike's and mine. Julianna IS for us. I called Mike at work and we agreed to meet at the hospital to see our daughter for the first time.

It was love at first sight for both of us. We knew immediately and without a single moment's doubt that God had delivered Julianna to us. Mike and I spent the next three months going back and forth to the hospital. Sometimes twice in a day. Each time I went to see Julianna, I would lay my hands upon her in her isolate and pray Psalms 139 and Jeremiah 1 over her. "Julianna, God knit you together in your mother's womb, you are fearfully and wonderfully made. God knows the plans He has for you, Julianna. They are plans for good and not for evil, you will live and not die."

Mike and I and all of our friends and family stood in faith for complete and perfect health for our baby girl. It was not an effortless or, faultless faith. Sometimes, I would cry all the way home from the hospital and ask Mike, "what if she does?" He would gently remind me of how God had pulled this together and that even if he did, God had planned for us to be her Mommy and Daddy. She needed us. Sometimes our friends and family would weaken, not so sure about just what we were getting into. We became very close to Julianna's doctors and her main nurse, Jayne. As we did, we learned more and more of the miracle details of her birth and her rescue from death. Not a single NICU team member could deny the miracle of her life or, her undefeatable spirit. Mike and I were always aware of what an honor and a privilege we had been given.

Julianna came home with us three months later. She had a head full of blonde hair, perfectly shaped tiny, rosy lips and beautiful pink skin. She was a perfectly healthy four pounds. No complications. No health problems. Nothing missing, nothing broken.

Today, Julianna is a beautiful young woman who loves God and loves life! How precious and great is our God!

So far you have:

Boldly stepped beyond fear and came forward to trust God with your secret pain.

Shared your secret.

Learned the truth about abortion and faced some difficult facts about the life of precious children lost to abortion.

Faced anger and unforgiveness of others involved in abortion

Looked into the face of your Lord to understand your own sin and receive His marvelous, mercy, grace and forgiveness

Now is the time for us to acknowledge and grieve those precious children lost to abortion.

It may seem odd, but it is really completely natural.

A dear friend of mine lost her firstborn child at birth. When the Doctor placed her stillborn baby girl in her arms for her to hold and say goodbye, he uttered some very wise words to my friend by telling her "before you can mourn her death, you must acknowledge her life".

In this step of the healing journey we are going to allow ourselves to do what our hearts have desired to do for a long time. God has led you to this place. He has held you and comforted you through each step of this very difficult journey. He has embraced you in his arms as you have come to terms with your anger and your grief. He is with you now and leading you as you acknowledge your grief and say good-bye to the children you, the entire world, has lost. We are at a crucial and special place in our healing journeys. This is the place where we can see our wounds healed, our broken hearts mended, and find reconciliation with our children. Here, we exchange bondage for freedom, fear for courage, and shame for enduring joy.

While this is a time of closure it is also a time of new beginnings. We can choose life. We can begin living in the light of God's redemptive healing.

Remember that you are God's child and are deeply loved by your Father. As you continue to face the loss of your child, you have permission to mourn, to accept comfort, and to comfort others who know the same pain that you have suffered.

Heart to Heart from Pat

Wow! The majesty of God is overwhelming. The victory found in our journey with God is well worth the process isn't it? We have made it to the top. I promised you at the beginning of this journey that we would get here and that you would be a different woman. Was I right? My guess is that God had done the most amazing things in your life over these past several weeks. That is not to say that all of the work that God is doing in your life is done. Oh no. God's work in us is a process. God will continue to heal your heart and show you more that He has for you. For several years after that first book encounter God continued to work out many things in my life, issues and attitudes that led to my abortion as well as the things that followed, bad decisions and choices. Each woman who shared her story with me brought out new things hidden in my heart that I had shoved aside or refused to admit.

Regardless of the timing or the individual process God uses, I have never taken anyone on this journey in over twenty years that I have not watched God change their life before my very eyes. It has been the most amazing privilege, one that I will be challenging you towards next chapter...we'll talk about that more later. But for now, even though I cannot see you, I am certain that your face is different than it was when you stepped into this dreaded mountain climb. You have accomplished so much. Do you remember the story of Esther in the Bible? I love that story. In fact, I have loved it so much over the years that I have transferred that love to my own daughter who now claims it as her favorite as well. The thing that I love most about Esther is her courage. She never signed up for her assignment, putting her pretty little neck on the line was not her idea of a good time, but God had a plan and she, in her obedience and her love for God, followed His plan, to the salvation of a nation. God has also had a plan for you. He chose you for this journey. He wants you healed and whole and ready to be given an assignment that will change that world, just like he did for Esther. But first, we have to end at the beginning. Remember how at the start of our journey, we had to understand how going back is sometimes required for moving forward? We are kind of at that place again.

Last chapter you ended with a bittersweet assignment. You

were asked to write a letter, a poem or a song, to your unborn child or children. I know that your heart is full of loss and sorrow over the child of your heart who is missing from your life. I know, I have a daughter who is standing with yours. God in His tender mercy allowed me to see her in that special way that we see things from God. She was whole and joyful. She was full of grace and mercy for me. I actually saw her reach out to me and comfort ME! Imagine that! I believe that you probably can. She assured me of her place with the Lord and her anticipation of the day that we would be together in heaven, the day that she would meet both her brothers and her own precious sister. You must know that you will never completely walk away from the longing to embrace that lost child, but also know, that God's grace is sufficient for you. He will give you an everlasting peace that when you think of your son or daughter, His peace is bigger than your grief and loss. Let God complete the work that He has begun in you, in His time. Trust Him, do not waver. Just Trust!

Surrender your life to Him and He will take you on a new journey that you would not believe even if you were told!

"Look at the nation and be utterly amazed for I am about to do something in your day that you would not believe, even if you were told" (Habakkuk 1:5).

Chapter Seven JOURNAL TIME

Take some time to write a letter to your unborn child or the children you are acknowledging. It may be your grandchild or your niece or nephew. Write them a letter expressing God's great love for all life created by Him and for Him. You may want to go to a sweet, quiet place and write a letter telling them of your sorrow and your love. Choose a flower or a memorial marker to leave in that place as you release your child to the loving hands of God. If you have surrendered your heart to Christ, you can rest assured that will see him or her again. You will hold your son or daughter in your arms and you will get back what the enemy intended to steal.

If there is someone you know who would understand this journey, make arrangements to share your letter with them. If you haven't done so before, NOW is the time to contact us at the Surrendering the Secret National office for help. In the meantime, let me pray for you.

Lord, I thank You for Your grace. I thank You that You work all things together for good for those who love You. I thank You for the deeper personal relationship that I now have with You. In my weakness I have found Your strength. I pray that You will place the desire in my heart to share this journey with other women and to reach out to them as You have reached out to me, sharing the freedom and joy that You have secured for us.

Before you move on, take some time to read and write out

God's plan for your future as you consider these truths.

Trust in the Lord with all your heart, and do not rely on your own understanding; think about Him in all your ways, and He will guide you on the right paths. (Proverbs 3:5-6, HCSB)

"For I know the plans I have for you," declares the Lord, "plans to prosper you and not to harm you, plans to give you hope and a future. Then you will call upon me and come and pray to me, and I will listen to you. You will seek me and find me when you seek me with all your heart. (Jeremiah 29:11-13, NIV)

What Jesus has done with your past failures and sins:

Surely our grief's He Himself bore, and our sorrows He carried; yet we ourselves esteemed Him stricken, smitten of God, and afflicted. But He was pierced through for our transgressions, He was crushed for our iniquities; the chastening for our well-being fell upon Him, and by His scourging we are healed. (Isaiah 53:4-5, NASB)

Let all that I am praise the Lord; may I never forget the good things he does for me. He forgives all my sins and heals all my diseases. He redeems me from death and crowns me with love and tender mercies. ... For his unfailing love toward those who fear him is as great as the height of the heavens above the earth. He has removed our sins as far from us as the east is from the west. The Lord is like a father to his children, tender and compassionate to those who fear him. (Psalm 103:2-4,11-13, NLT)

Life ...

Remember that we have settled many truths about what

the Bible has to say about life:

- **Not only is your child fully human from the moment of conception, but also he or she has already been given a personal, eternal soul.**
- **All prenatal existence is linked to a postnatal life. The life of our soul is an eternal spiritual continuum that begins at conception and continues into eternity.**
- **God placed inestimable value on your child from the moment of conception; he or she was created and deeply loved by God.**

At death, the unborn child immediately passes into the presence of God. Each little one is present with the Father. They have identity and individuality, they deserve to be known for who they are: eternal beings. They still have a divine purpose which, though it may transcend our understanding for the moment, we shall perceive clearly when the day dawns that we no longer see through a glass darkly but then will see face to face.

Read the story of David and Bathsheba found in 2 Samuel 11 and 12. This is the story of a man whose sin led to the loss of his son. He, like us, was the reason the child did not survive. He was also called "a man after God's own heart," a man who understood his own failure and repented of it. This is our story as well. David's God is our God; his promises are our promises. Listen to what the Bible says about seeing your child again someday:

King David replied, "I fasted and wept while the child was alive, for I said, 'Perhaps the LORD will be gracious to me and let the child live.' But why should I fast when he is dead? Can I bring him back again? I will go to him one day, but he cannot return to me." (2 Samuel 12:22-23, NLT 5)

Do not be afraid, for I am with you; I will bring your children from the east and gather you from the west. I will say to the north, "Give them up!" and to the south, "Do not hold them back." Bring my sons from afar and my daughters from the ends of the earth— everyone who is called by my name, whom I created for my glory, whom I formed and made." (Isaiah 43:5-7, NIV)

JOURNAL TIME

_____

_____

_____

_____

_____

_____

_____

_____

_____

_____

_____

_____

_____

_____

_____

_____

_____

_____

_____

_____

_____

_____

_____

_____

_____

_____

JOURNAL TIME

_____

_____

_____

_____

_____

_____

_____

_____

_____

_____

_____

_____

_____

_____

_____

_____

_____

_____

_____

_____

_____

_____

_____

_____

_____

_____

8

Passing It On!

I stepped from my house into my garage with a giant bag of hand-me-down clothes to share with my younger sister. As I stepped through the door I was caught by the sound of men's voices and strained by tears. I quickly discovered my husband and our middle son sitting in the middle of our garage huddled in a heap of tears. It took me a minute to register in my head what I was seeing. They were supposed to be mowing the lawn for goodness sakes. What in the world had happened?

I soon discovered that the two of them had somehow landed in a discussion about the abortion my husband and I had so many years before. My husband was set to join me in sharing our testimony at an upcoming event for our local pregnancy center ministry. We had always shared openly with our children about these past choices. All three of them had been raised with the open sharing, speaking and writing God had called me into.

At the time of this encounter our son was about seventeen and had apparently asked my husband some clarifying questions about what all had happened. As my son listened to his Dad reflect upon his heartbreak, he began for the first time to embrace his own personal loss of a baby sister. You might imagine what came down on our garage floor that day as the three of us wept and grieved afresh, the loss of an innocent part of our family.

On that day two things happened that changed me forever. One, God healed my heart just a little bit more and two, I made a fresh commitment to Him to share with anyone, anytime He asked me to so that the next generation, my son and his children would not buy the same lie his Dad and I had fallen for.

I am committed to challenging and encouraging women and men who have had past abortions to seek healing; to understand God's redeeming love; then to openly share the truth so that our children and grandchildren will be spared this holocaust.

Just like the bag of "hand-me-down" clothes that were headed to my sister that one life changing morning, we can and do pass on what we have not cleaned up! Let's clean this up for those coming after us. Let's tell them the truth. The word of OUR testimony is THEIR only hope.

We have traveled an amazing journey together. We are not the same people who came together when you first picked up this book. We are not the same women who were afraid of what we might find in its pages and afraid to face the truth and pain of the dark secret of abortion. God has been good. He has begun a powerful work of healing in us, and He has brought us to a new time and place. Even though the path ahead is unfamiliar we're ready to move forward into all He has in store for us.

Your Ongoing Journey

As we close our journey together, please realize that completing a book full of steps doesn't mean your journey is completed. It's actually just beginning. This time has been only one chapter in YOUR story.

All the days ordained for me were written in your book before one of the came to be. (Psalm 139:16, NIV)

You've kept track of my every toss and turn through the sleepless nights, each tear entered in your ledger, each ache written in our book...I'm proud to praise God, proud to praise God. Fearless now, I trust in God: what can mere mortals do to me? God, you did everything you promised, and I'm thanking you with all my heart. You pulled me from the brink of death, my felt from the cliff edge of doom. Now I stroll at leisure with God in the sunlit fields of life. (Psalm 56:8, 10-13 The Message)

God is calling you into a great adventure. He has a unique role just for you. As you step outside yourself to engage in the larger story, acknowledge that completing the first pass through the eight steps doesn't mean there's nothing for you. Here's some of what Goad has in store for you as you continue the journey with Him:

I (God) will restore the years the swarming locust has eaten, the crawling locust, the consuming locust, and the chewing locust. (Joel 2-25 NKJV)

Locusts are ravenous, devouring life as they swarm. In this passage, locusts represent the torment or consequences that have come in to our lives as result of bad decisions we or other people have made. In our case, they clearly represent the pain of abortions that has chewed up our lives and relationships.

I pray that out of his glorious riches he may strengthen you with power through his Spirit and your inner being, so that Christ may dwell in your hearts through faith. And I pray that you, being rooted and established in love, may have power, together with all the saints, to grasp how wide and long and high and deep is the love of Christ, and to know this love that surpasses knowledge—that you may be filled to the measure of all the fullness of God. Now to him who is able to do immeasurable more than all we ask or imagine, according to his power that is a work within us, to him be glory in the church and in Christ Jesus throughout all generations, forever and ever! Amen (Ephesians 3-16 21, NIV)

We speak of Gods' secret wisdom a wisdom that has been hidden and that God destined for our glory before time began...as it is written: "No eye has seen, nor ear has heard, not mind has conceived what God has prepared for those who love him." (1 Corinthians 2-7:9, NIV)

The Power of Your Story

God's provisions for the past are not only sufficient, but His promises for our future are incredibly bright! God invites us to become instruments of His love. His life, and His healing power. God has led us on a path of healing; now He wants to use our stories to help others. Our goal now must be to discover and pursue God's purposes for our lives.

Revelation 12:11 shows the end of our stories as it talks about the larger story and the coming final battle between good and evil.

"They overcome him by the blood of the Lamb (Jesus), and by the word of their testimony they did not love their lives so much as to shrink away for earth." (Revelation 12:11)

In Revelation 12:11, "they" refers to us, Jesus' followers. "Him" who will be overcome refers to the enemy. What three things are crucial in overcoming the work of the enemy? How can our stories or testimonies be powerful in the battle?

I (God) will restore the years the swarming locust has eaten, the crawling locust, the consuming locust, and the chewing locust.
Joel 2-25 NKJV

Live Your Story

Remember these three key truths as you pursue your role in the larger story.

Key 1: God wants us to live for something greater than ourselves!

For everything, absolutely everything, above and below, visible and invisible, rank after rank after rank of angels — everything got stared in him and finds its purpose in him. (Colossians 1-16, The Message)

I chose you before I formed you in the womb; I set you apart before you were born. I appointed you a prophet to the nations. (Jeremiah 1-5, HCSB)

Key 2: We are saved to serve God! We are healed to serve others!

Don't be ashamed of the testimony about our Lord, or of me His prisoner. Instead, share in the suffering for the gospel, relying on the power of God, who has saved us and called us with a hold calling, not according to our works, but according to His own purpose and grace, which was given to us in Christ Jesus before time began. (2 Timothy 18-9 HCSB)

Do you not know that your body is a sanctuary for the Holy Spirit who is in you, whom you have from God? You are not your own, for were bought at a price; therefore glorify God in your body. (1 Corinthians 6 19-20, HCSB)

Key 3 God's power is revealed in on our weakness.

Brothers, consider your calling: not many are wise from a human perspective, not many powerful, not many of noble birth. Instead, God has chosen the world's foolish things to shame the wise, and God has chosen the world's weak things to shame the strong. God has chosen the world's insignificant and despised things the things viewed as nothing so He might bring to nothing the things that are viewed as something, so that no one can boast in His presence. But from Him you are in Christ Jesus, who for us became wisdom from God as well as righteousness, sanctification, and redemption. (I Corinthians 1:26-30 HCSB)

Setting Hearts Free

As we learn to accept and appreciated who we really are in Him and who He really is in us, God has an adventure waiting for us.

Read Isaiah 61:1-3 aloud, replacing "me" with your name.

The Spirit of the Sovereign Lord is on me, because the Lord has anointed me to preach good news to the poor. He has sent me to bind up the brokenhearted, to proclaim freedom for the captives and release from darkness for the prisoners, to proclaim the year of the Lord's favor and the day of vengeance of our God, to comfort al who mourn and provide for those who grieve in Zion-to bestow on them a crown of beauty instead of ashes, the oil of gladness instead of mourning, and a garment of praise instead of a spirit of despair. (Isaiah 61:1-3 NIV)

As you join with Jesus in His mission to bind up the brokenhearted, set captives free, and replace beauty for ashes, you won't' believe how exciting and deeply fulfilling that can be!

Bless be the God and Father of our Lord Jesus Christ, the Father of mercies and the God of all comfort. He comforts us in all our affliction, so that we may be able to comfort those who are in any kind of affliction; through the comfort we ourselves receive from God. For as the sufferings of Christ overflow to us, so our comfort overflows through Christ. (2 Corinthians 1:3-5 HCSB)

But thanks be to God, who always leads us in triumph in Christ, ad manifests through us the sweet aroma of the knowledge of Him in every place. For we are a fragrance of Christ to God among those who are being saved and among those who are perishing to the one aroma from death to death, to the other an aroma from life to life. And who is adequate for these things? 2 Corinthians 2 14-16, HCSB

Some Thoughts to Ponder

How is God the Father portrayed in 2 Corinthians 1:3 and 2:14? How does this portrayal compare to your deepest heart beliefs about God?

According to I Corinthians 1-26-30, what kind of people does God chose to use for His rescue mission in our world? What turns people like us into heroes (verse 30)?

How do you think your past wounds and brokenness enhance your usefulness to God and His work of comforting, healing, and setting captives free? (2 Corinthians 1:4-5)

What world—changing challenges is placed before us in 2 Corinthians 2:15-16? How would your answer Paul's question: "Who is adequate for these things?"

Look again at these two passages from the perspective of what you receive, rather than what you give. What are the benefits to your own recovery and healing as you share with others and become God's "triumph" a "sweet aroma"? (2 Corinthians 1:4-5; 2:15-16)

The amazing thing is that as your work with Jesus in setting captives free, you'll find that one of the captives that's becoming more increasingly liberated is you! God has made some amazing promises to us if we are willing to raise our eyes to Him (above our current pain) and embrace the larger story. These promises give powerful incentive no to give up, but to continue on to still more.

Thousands of women and men, bound by secret abortions, are sitting in our churches, living as our neighborhoods, and they may even be our closest friends. Your sharing could help set the f free. As Revelation 12:11 illustrates, unmatchable power lies in your willingness to be vulnerable.

Using wisdom and prayer to guide your sharing in very important. God will show you how when, where, and with whom. God would not have you injure or hurt others in the process of sharing.

As we close this time that we have spent together, my sincere and heartfelt prayer is that we are someday soon to meet, face to face.

Heart to Heart from Pat

I have to tell you that as we close this time that we have spent together, my sincere and heartfelt prayer is that we are someday soon to meet, face to face.

I have been married to the same man for over thirty-six years. We have three children, five grandchildren and two beautiful daughters by marriage to our sons. We have family in heaven including our daughter lost to abortion and a grandson lost just before his birth. We have a marriage that has survived purely by God's grace.

God has used us despite the ugliness of our past, the bad choices and the constant failures of our lives to make a difference in the lives of others...prayerfully in your life!

I am a woman who is living my story. God wants the same thing from each one of us. He wants our story!!

Revelation 12:11 says that we overcome the work of the enemy in three ways; there are no other ways to get him outside of these three.

Number 1: The precious atoning blood of Jesus. Nothing surpasses that. He alone is our Savior, our redeemer, our merciful Lord. He is our one and only, our all in all!

Number 2: Second only to Jesus, is the word of our testimony. Our stories, yours, and mine are what God uses to establish His Kingdom here on earth. Imagine that ladies. Not only does our Lord rescue us and remove our sin but also he wants us to be part of His salvation message to the world. It is more than my little brain can really understand but it is true. I have lived it, I have seen it. The fact that you are reading my book today is not less than a miracle, the level or parting the red sea and raising people from the dead. Never in my wildest hopes or dreams would this be happening. Not only because of my past sin but also because of my ever present and daily failures! God continues to show me that His WORD means business. He wants to use broken but surrendered women. I believe that you are one of those women.

Number 3: The last way the scripture says that we overcome Satan's plans is to "not love and cling to our lives even when faced with death". I am not a Bible scholar and have read many studies of Revelation Chapter 12. The book in its entirety fascinates me as John uses the analogy of a woman and her child in the final battle against the enemy. Someday, I will take the time to pursue Gods' interpretation of those words for women today, but for now, I have come to understand that last part of Revelation 12:11 to mean that I must be willing to SURRENDER the life that I might think I want for myself. I have to be willing to symbolically "die" to some of the things that think I want for my life, some of the things that other people think I should do with my life. I have to let that all go, for the number one thing God has called me to do with my life and that is to live my story through the word of my testimony, spoken, written, shared one on one. The fact that abortion is law of the land, that most churches have no voice against it and that women and men are hidden in their own shame and secrets is surely a heartbreak to our God.

We must tell someone.

We must reach out to our silent sisters and brothers and draw them out.

We must be willing to tell our stories so that others can be healed and set free. I have watched what God has done with women who are set free just by my own transparency, my own story. Free men and women change the world. I want to encourage you to prayerfully consider what God would have you do with this healing in your life. Consider starting a Surrendering the Secret Bible Study in your church or sharing your testimony at a ladies' retreat, writing it out for your church newsletter or taking your story to your local CPC for them to use with other women. Talk to your Pastor, your women's ministry leader or your church's counseling Pastor. Tell someone what God has done. DO not let the enemy hold your secret any longer.

As we part, I hope to hear from you, by email or via our several social media locations.

stsinternational15@gmail.com

I want to hear how your journey has progressed and what God is doing with your ministry of restoration.

Let me close our work together with the words that ring most loudly in my heart with this ministry and with what I truly see God doing in this process in all of our lives.

"Now to Him, who by the power that is at work within US, sisters, me and you, is able to carry out His purposes and do supernaturally far over and above, all that we dare ask or think, infinitely beyond our highest prayers, desires, thoughts, hopes or dreams. To Him be the Glory in the church and in Christ Jesus throughout all generations forever and ever, Amen." (Eph 3:20,21)

Chapter Eight JOURNAL TIME

What cautions you might need to exercise as you begin to share your story with others? Consider your motives. Be sensitive and ask God how to wait for His leading in sharing your abortion experience before you step out publicly.

With whom might you speak privately before sharing your abortion publicly? Your husband? Parents? Your children know? By being brave and trusting God you may save one of them from making the same choice.

Brainstorm ways with someone you trust that you can use your healing from abortion to reach out to other women who are hurting and still in bondage.

Establish some sort of accountability about how you will serve God in helping others as you have been helped. Remember the statistics from chapter three indicated 43% of women of childbearing age have been broken by abortion. Only the truth, that you now have, can help set them free.

How willing are you to participate in the adventure of setting hearts free? What if any reservations do you have?

What unique gifts, talents, resources, and life experience has God given you to comfort hurting people, to release them from bondage, or to show them the way to Jesus so they can find redemption from shame and failures?
How might people respond to your encouragement that there is a way out of their problems, pain and destructive behaviors?

Continually review chapter six to remind yourself of God's promise to you. Keep God's Word in your mouth an in your heart. Remember, we have decided to choose life!
Think back to the first time you opened this book.

You'll remember that the common thread you have shared with thousands of women and men was the experience of a past abortion. It is that painful experience that connects you. Thousands more could identify with you as a result of that experience. They need you.

Now that you have completed your journey, you can identify with others in a new way.
You are SET FREE by threads of forgiveness, hope, and grace.

You are woman of courage who has climbed a mountain of strength and courage. Your identity is no longer that of pos-abortive woman or man. You are child of God, of truth and integrity and your identity is in Christ and who He says you are. You are new creation in Christ. The abortion that appeared to be a mountain from below is now under your feet. God has been faithful to do what He said He would do. He has set the captives free. He has set YOU FREE!

Although you've completed *A Surrendered Life*, the rest of your life is a continuing journey with Christ. In life, there will always mountains to climb until we reach our heavenly destination. So, as you go forward, be good to yourself, take time to love yourself, smile inwardly, and keep your sense of humor.

My love and blessings, Pat

JOURNAL TIME

SECTION TWO

The Ripple Effect of Abortion
Men, Couples and Families

Sharing with Your Children

Over the past many years of watching women walk the journey of healing through Surrendering the Secret, the most common roadblock for using a past abortion as a Revelation 12;11 opportunity—the word of our testimony, is the fear of telling our children about our past abortions.

Let me tell you my friend. We must tell.

Friends, we must be willing, in God's timing, to tell our precious sons and daughters that we are sinners saved by grace.

We may just discover a whole new level of love come from our transparency and surrender to God's leading.

If we want to save our children from making our same mistakes, we must tell.

Let me start with a recent article I wrote about my own challenges with this very topic.

"What is this book, G," my oldest granddaughter asked from her seat behind me in the car.

My heart dropped. I'd forgotten I'd left some of my Surrendering the Secret books in a basket on the floorboard of my car. As a brand-new reader, she grabbed everything with writing on it to test out her newfound skill.

"It has your name on it. Did you write this, G?"

"Yes, I did, it's a Bible Study."

"Can we read it?"

"Yes, someday I'll read it to you, beautiful girl"

Oh my. Someday, I will have to talk to my precious, adorable granddaughter about my abortion. Someday, I will have to tell her about my sin, my loss, and my restoration through Jesus. Someday, but not today.

It has been forty years since abortion on-demand became the law of the land in the United States, after the Supreme Court ruled 5-4 in favor of the plaintiff in Roe v. Wade. In those forty years, 55 million unborn American babies have become fatalities of abortion.

The Bible places particular significance on the number forty. The pages of Scripture are filled with events and people whose stories are marked off by that number, which represents a generation.

Consider Moses and the Israelites, who wandered forty years in the wilderness just outside of the Promise Land, until the old, rebellious generation was gone and a new generation arose to take its place.

What a humbling concept, as we consider the shedding of innocent blood—which God hates (Proverbs 6:17)—that has been legally endorsed over the past forty years. America has lost nothing less than a generation.

For my part, I am missing a daughter, along with nieces and nephews, precious children of friends and friends I'll never know because they were never allowed to take a breath on this earth.

Little did I know the devastation and loss of innocent life that would be the result of my articles, petitions, and politics. Little did I know that my own ignorance and selfishness would lead me to opt for abortion.

Little did I know that my own precious firstborn daughter would be one of those lost lives. Little did I know that someday, I would have to share that story with my own granddaughter.

I am passionate, vocal, and pro-choice. However, this time, my message of CHOICE declares the words of Deut. 30:19:

> *I have set before you life and death—choose life so that you and your children may live.*

I am now counting on a new promise, found in Revelation 12:11, which assures me that we Christians conquer even our worst enemies—even Satan himself—by "the blood of the Lamb and by the word of (our) testimony."

It has become my life's passion and calling to do all I can to protect and defend the next generation.

Maybe I will read it to my granddaughter. Someday.

Another Mother/Daughter Story of the Power of Forgiveness

The most difficult journey is back to the place where you failed. So difficult, that I had managed to avoid that journey for over twenty-five years! Suddenly I was there; the journey quick, to an unexpected, unplanned (by me) **moment of truth...**

Jenni, my young adult daughter, and I had met at Starbuck's to plan a Girl's Weekend for the Senior High students I was teaching at my church. We were going to study with them a book titled, "When God Writes Your Love Story." In the middle of our planning, (in the middle of Starbucks!), she just put her pen down, faced me with a look that portrayed surprise, confidence, even expectancy, and said, "Mom, I can't seem to shake an overwhelming sense that there's something *you* need to tell me."

Well, my heart started racing in about a million different directions, but my mind was stayed on what I knew God was doing. You see, I had prayed for this moment, a chance to tell her, but now? *Not now!* In my mind, I wrestled with God for what seemed liked hours before I managed to open my mouth and speak.

Body trembling and tears falling, I began sharing my secret story. "Well, Honey, you remember that I told you a few years ago, because you asked, that your Dad and I had indeed had sex *before* we were married? Well, I have managed to skirt around the rest of the story____ until now.   ...The rest of the story being that I got pregnant, and____ well, there is no baby, so you can probably guess what happened."

Her reply? "No, Mom, I can't guess; I have no idea what

happened." God was going to make *me* say the 'word', sure enough! Eyes downcast with shame and giant tears falling by now, I spoke the truth: "At age eighteen, I had an abortion."

Expecting horror in her eyes, I saw love. Waiting for the words, *Mom, how could you!?*, I heard instead, "Mom, I'm so sorry you went through that." And then she said, "Mom, this just explains so much!"

Truth brings understanding! Suddenly pieces of life made sense to her; things like my nervous reactions to her teenage years, especially her dating years, mine and her Dad's marriage problems, our almost divorcing, our fights, and so much more. And when *I* heard her words I realized that abortion had affected every part of my life. I also knew, without a doubt, that it was God who had prompted her question, and it was He who had journeyed me to this moment, this *surrendering of my secret.*

In a beautiful card Jenni sent me the very next week she wrote: "Mom, for as long as I have been alive, you have given yourself and more for me. The one thing I could not ask of you, because I did not know to ask of you, was for your TRUTH." That precious daughter, gift from God, *thanked* me for sharing what I needed to release, what she needed to hear!

Telling the TRUTH set me free!

Truth set us BOTH free to love the Word of God together, to grow and share and speak truth to others!

"Let's tell them, she said, Tell them we are NOT slaves to fear/ guilt/ sin. WE ARE FREE!" Can I hear a Hallelujah?

God started a journey that day, using my own precious daughter to display the kind of love and freedom He had waiting for me. He drew the truth out of me. He journeyed me back to the place I had failed, not to shame me, but to free me from its grip on my past, my present and my future! And the journey continued, taking me places where I would discover there was such a thing as Post Abortion healing Bible studies, namely, *Surrendering the Secret*. This Bible study solidified that telling my truth, and trusting God's truth, transforms us all! Now, as a leader of this study, I call *Surrendering the Secret* a "trust journey" through God's Word over the soul wound of abortion.

"We overcome by the blood of the Lamb and the word of our testimony!" (Rev 12:11)

I am overwhelmed that God has used the deepest shame of my life to demonstrate to me the true mercy of the Cross and to ignite in me a passion to share the truth that surrendering to Him empowers and frees!

Tricia Heflin,

Surrendering the Secret National Leader, Texas

The Daughter's Story

In just a few short weeks, my amazing hubby and I will be celebrating eight incredible years of life as ONE! What an insane, wild, fun, scary, exhilarating, BLESSED ride it has truly been! God has never abandoned us, not for one single second. He has faithfully carried us through amazing seasons as well as heart breaking ones. Through growth and hurt and confusion to hope and exceedingly great joy and promise! He sure writes the best stories doesn't He?

Shortly after Chris and I were married, God planned and incredible moment for my Mom and I. It was a surprise encounter, and an experience that would change BOTH of us for the better. We were planning a girls' retreat together at a coffee shop just down the street from my house. We always have such a blast together and this was no exception! As we dreamed and planned, however I could not shake the sense that there was something blocking our conversation. I specifically felt the Lord leading me to ask her if there was something she needed to tell me.

"I had an abortion." Those four little words fell reluctantly out of the mouth of the LAST person I would have EVER expected to hear them from. It's actually quite hard for me to even remember her being so afraid to speak those words out loud. The boldness she has now to tell any and everyone who will listen is truly remarkable and an absolute miracle! I know telling her daughter was perhaps one of the most difficult, but crucial steps toward her journey to freedom. The enemy had convinced her rejection would surely follow such a confession. However, nothing could be farther from the truth. The truth always empowers and *frees* us! Not only did I feel immediate compassion and love for my mom, I also felt a strange understanding come over me in regards to my own life. As the truth was setting her free, it also set me free.

All of a sudden, I began to make sense of so many of the things in my life I could never understand before. Why she felt the need to over-protect me from everything, my own struggles to stay pure, and countless other decisions she made in raising me that had been guided by the guilt of her secret. Our relationship was strengthened as a result of her confessions as well, because I finally knew she wasn't as perfect as I had originally thought. Capable of sin and in need of forgiveness, just like me. It was an incredible moment God had planned for us, and a conversation I will treasure forever!

Since then, I have watched God redeem her story and use it to set so many countless others free as well. Honestly, as a mother of three, I now feel the tragedy and heartbreak of abortion at a much deeper level. Falling in love with your children will do that to you. I understand her pain so much more, and pray for God to use her story to save others from such a choice. Whatever place in life this finds you, may you know that you are never too far out of His reach. Love and grace are just a prayer away. *Freedom* awaits you. LIFE, that is truly life (Jude 21) lies on the other side of surrender.

Jenni,

The very proud daughter

SHARING WITH YOUR CHILDREN

"Mommy had an abortion"

By Kelly Clinger

Those are words I never thought I would say to my children. *In fact, I was never going to tell them.* I didn't want to explain what abortion was much less tell them that their own mother had made such a terrible, sinful choice... TWICE.

When I was asked to be a spokesperson for the Silent No More Awareness Campaign toward the end of 2010, they wanted to be sure that my immediate family knew my past before I began traveling the country talking about it. Of course my husband knew most of the details (although more things surface as time goes on), *but how was I going to tell my kids that I killed two of their siblings?*

My daughter was fourteen and my son was eight at the time. I didn't want them to be disappointed in me. I didn't want them to hate me. *I didn't want them to feel about me the way I felt about myself.*

I sat the kids down on the couch and took a deep breath. I asked them if they knew what abortion was. My daughter said she had heard the word before but wasn't sure what it was. My son was clueless. As I began to explain it, the horror was all over their faces. *"How could anyone do that?"* my son asked. He kept asking questions, but my daughter's silence told me that she knew there was a reason I was talking to them about abortion.

I began to cry and said, *"Mommy had two abortions ten years ago. You have two siblings in heaven."*

I am crying now thinking about the shock and the disappointment on their little faces. It felt like the Mommy they knew wasn't who they thought she was. I wonder about all of the questions that raced through their heads during those few seconds...all of the things that they may be able to articulate years from now but can't process in their young minds now.

My daughter scooted closer to me and threw her arms around me. "*I forgive you, Mom...it's ok*", she said. "*I do too*", my son said, "*and when I get older, I'm NEVER going to let my wife do that.*" We all cried together.

I went on to tell them about praying and asking God if the babies were boys or girls and what He would like me to name them. I told them about how God said they were both girls and we had named them Goodness and Mercy. "*Like the Bible verse!*" my son shouted.

That was almost two years ago, and they've heard Mommy talk about Goodness and Mercy a lot now. Anytime we hear a song with Psalm 23 in it or someone reads that scripture, my son will proudly announce, "*Those are my sisters!*" Abortion is a common topic around our dinner table. I joined the fight for LIFE by myself, but we now fight together as a family.

As Mother's Day approaches, many feel the sting of loss, but along with the sting, I feel the guilt. I will have two Mother's Day cards missing...my breakfast in bed will be prepared by 2 children instead of four. There is a void that will not be filled until I see Jesus face to face, but until then my hope remains in this: "*Surely goodness and mercy shall follow me all the days of my life...*"

FROM A FATHER'S HEART

Abortion hurts men too. As more women respond to the healing journey of a past abortion, God is clearly stirring the hearts of men across the nation as well. At the national headquarters of Surrendering the Secret, calls come in on a regular basis seeking someone to talk to who understands the loss of Fatherhood caused by abortion. Abortion is the antithesis to all God created, called, equipped, and empowered men to do and experience in life!

Men really want to provide for and protect others, especially their women and children. Most men tend to fix things, stuff things, and control things yet they also want to succeed and accomplish things.

How do men deal and cope with a past abortion? The answer is in multiple ways! Men experience many emotions and start acting out in multiple ways to deal with the pain, guilt, and grief and inability to protect their child including:

- Stuffing feelings
- Drinking
- Anxiety
- Withdrawing
- No Relationships
- Drugging
- Depression
- Cynicism
- Multiple unhealthy relationships
- No motivation to excel
- Feeling like failure
- Low self-worth
- Disdain for women

Men who originally agreed with or even pressed for abortion often bury their feelings and behavior by justifying their decision. Not so different from women, here are a few common rationalizations:

· It was legal and best for everyone

· We can't afford a child right now

· Everybody has abortions, it's not a big deal

· The timing wasn't right to get married

· We hardly knew each other

In most cases it's not easy for men to join other men they don't know to pursue post abortion recovery. It's difficult at first to open up about their past behaviors or share their feelings and thoughts and participate in a post-abortion group. It takes a great deal of courage and humility for a man to submit to a group setting and make himself vulnerable emotionally and spiritually.

When they do, in a short period of time trust and bonding build, and honest dialogue of sharing feelings and emotions are expressed. Some men share more openly, easily and at times passionately while others suppress their feelings, "fighting" instead of dealing with their pent-up emotions.

After a few weeks, tears appear, deep personal feelings are being shared instead of trying to avoid or fix others, hardened hearts and offenses begin softening and evidence of the healing process can occur through the power of the Holy Spirit.

For some men the healing is deeper and more profound earlier in the group process than other men. God... is at work transforming each of their hearts filling these men with hope, wisdom, and discernment and bringing to the surface a repentant spirit and confession of sin. It is a life changing experience to watch 1 John 1:9 come to life on the faces of these men.

"When you confess your sin, God is faithful and just to forgive your sin and cleanse you of all unrighteousness."

As trust, confidence and insight build, the men start questioning and confronting one another. In most cases this is done lovingly and respectfully and received very well. As they begin to operate as a team, building unity and praying for each other, the healing process takes place.

Conversation and interaction increase, stuffed memories and emotions are released, and detailed personal experiences and testimonies are shared.

Men don't like to fail or feel helpless, hopeless, trapped, out of control or let others down especially family, friends and an unborn child! When a man experiences an abortion that he did not want to happen, everything inside him cries out, "Failure!" Since he wasn't able to save and protect his child, anger and resentment begin to build. Anger is caused by:

- Hurt
- Fear
- Shame
- Injustice
- Offense
- Frustration

When men take the time to complete each chapter of Surrendering the Secret they are filled with Scripture, self-revealing questions and truth that sets the free from guilt and shame. Greater and deeper signs of healing and forgiveness are revealed to the point that the men more transparent, about thither things in life and experience God's love and grace. Transformation takes place in these men through the power of the Holy Spirit helping them to fulfill God's calling and destiny in their lives. In the end they feel forgiven and empowered experiencing the Joy of the Lord!

COUPLES AND ABORTION

Statistics indicate that it is a rare occurrence for a couple to survive an abortion decision. By the grace of God, some do, including me and my husband Mike. Our healing journey through a past abortion was a long and tender one. God has brought us a long way as we have now celebrated four decades of marriage and served together in this ministry for close to thirty of those years. The work of healing through such a painful choice as abortion is certainly not an easy one--but God! His promises sustain us, and His healing love allows us to see our failures as small compared to His power and plans. Trust Him to lead your journey as well.

I pray that these stories of redemption encourage you.

Jenn and Anthony

Anthony: Nine years after our abortion, I saw an announcement in our church's bulletin about *Surrendering the Secret*; I wanted to talk to Jen about it, but I didn't know how to bring it up. It was something we'd hidden, even from each other, for almost a decade.

Jen: After I registered, I knew I'd have to tell Anthony, mostly because I'd need him to watch our kids so I could go. I was really afraid to talk to him about it. I wasn't scared of his reaction; it was a fear of saying "abortion" out loud, of admitting that we'd had one, but mostly I needed help to heal from its devastation. That's how much of a secret I had let it become. I couldn't even say the word to my husband.

Anthony: I remember when she told me she was going to the STS study; I felt relieved, even glad. We sat in the car, at a stop sign, and I asked Jen if I could come, too.

Jen: He held my hand when he asked. That was the first time we had ever talked about the abortion. Anthony's words really started to make this a safe discussion to have. It let me know that Anthony was hurting from our abortion, too. That was something I'd never considered before, the fact that our abortion had wounded Anthony as well.

Anthony: As Jen went through, we would talk about the different steps she was on. In the beginning, that was key: talking about this event that had preceded our marriage and this secret that was really the foundation on which our marriage was based. I began to see, as she moved through the process, that I also needed healing personally; and so did our marriage.

Jen: Anthony's support and prayers not only carried me through the study but gave me the freedom to really deal with the devastation our abortion caused. I began to see the damage our abortion had inflicted on our marriage. We both discovered that we were harboring deep resentment and unforgiveness towards one another.

Anthony: That bitterness effected how we lived as a couple. I often felt distant from Jen and would emotionally separate myself from her. I didn't see her as a safe person to talk to; and this led me to keep secrets from her.

Jen: Every day since our abortion, I felt that Anthony was running away from me, emotionally, in actual geographic distance, and spiritually. Even after we got married, I never felt completely connected to him. There was a real chasm between us, and I kept trying to cross it and reach him; but I never could. That lack of oneness created deep bitterness in me. Eventually, I wound up pushing Anthony away so this emotional separation would hurt less.

Anthony: As Jen and then I uncovered the root of these feelings, through STS, we were able to really face and deal with them. We were able to recognize our anger and let it go in exchange for grace.

Jen: We were able to see our unforgiveness towards each other and, with Christ's help, extend forgiveness to each other. These experiences let us connect emotionally and spiritually, in a way and with a depth, that had never been a reality for us before.

Anthony: Also, we were finally able to grieve the loss of our child. Together. As her parents. I was emotionally weak during the grieving process and was able to lean on Jen for strength and encouragement. This was a point of genuine growth in our marriage for us to be able to be there and show our love and support for one another.

Jen: Through STS, we found grace for ourselves and for each other. We forgave one another and let go of years of bitterness. We had a unity in our marriage that had not existed before; we even started dreaming about doing ministry together! Through this study, God enabled us to come together as a couple and build a new foundation for our broken marriage; one based on truth, transparency, trust, and above all, on the grace of Jesus Christ.

Tricia and Steve

By the time I was leading *Surrendering the Secret* classes, I had begun to share publicly that abortion was true of me and share about the healing power of God's Word. I had told my story of abortion to our children and most family members. While my husband, Steve, was not exactly thrilled, he was "ok" with it.

God had done such a healing work in my life through *Surrendering the Secret*; I felt free! Free in a way I'd never understood *before*... Free from guilt and shame. Forgiven. Cleansed. Redeemed!

The experience of telling the TRUTH, surrendering the *secret* of abortion and exposing it to God's light of truth, created in me a freedom I couldn't keep to myself. While I was able to share with many other women, I so longed for my husband and I to be in this "together." We'd certainly chosen abortion together, but also together, had hidden this secret for over twenty-five years. *Hidden* was still a comfortable place for Steve. He seemed fine with letting it be *my issue* and now, it seemed, fine with letting it be *my healing*.

"Each heart knows its own bitterness, and no one else can share its joy." (Proverbs 14:10)

The first time I heard this Bible verse I thought, "That's it!... Steve will *never* truly understand what I went through and what pain I feel in my heart over the abortion." While I took comfort in that verse, trusting that God understood, even inspired this verse that helped me, I longed for Steve to *get it*, at least a little. Over three years of my leading *Surrendering the Secret* Bible study groups, volunteering as a counselor at a Pregnancy Center, and speaking whenever possible about this healing journey, Steve couldn't help but notice the changes in *his wife*. To mention a few: Confidence, kindness, increased faith, joy, closer relationship with our children and their support of this ministry. But every time I asked, "Will you do this study with me?" NO! "Will you watch the videos?" NO! "Men don't like to talk about it", was the explanation. I kept praying and trusting.

One day I received an email announcement that *Surrendering the Secret* was being offered as an online Couple's study! We would meet via *Skype* each week. Another married couple with abortion in their past would be leading it. I forwarded the message to Steve. NO! A few weeks went by: I prayed and re-sent the message with a few added words from my own heart. He came in from work that day and said, "I got your message. And OK! YES! I believe GOD is telling me to do this study with you."

Thank You, God! :-) We started the next week!

One of the first questions asked of us was, "What led you to this study?" Steve said, that for the past *three* years, he had watched me lead class after class, and come home "on cloud nine" about women changing and what God was doing in their lives. He heard the Word of God practically pour out of me. He saw changes in me and in others like he'd never seen from the many other Bible studies I'd taught, or the Bible studies he and I had taught together. "Abortion was indeed our choice *together* and it was time he said Yes to me instead of NO!" Steve's hope was that we would grow closer through this study. That happened, yes, but also, Steve began to see that God knows and cares about every detail of our lives and that trust in His Word changes us and brings new freedom.

As we began the study, Steve expressed, "This is a woman's study!" God gave him a new perspective on what it's like for women to read the Bible: Even though most all verses are written to "he" and about "him", not "her," women still have no doubt the Bible was written for them, as well as for men!

And Week Two: "Abortion story? I don't have an abortion

story." But as he worked through the pages of the study, Steve realized that he too had an "abortion story," not just me. He remembered not only the events, the clinic, the feelings, but even *thoughts* he'd had so long ago. He wrote, "I remember the long drive home thinking, this is *it* between us. Look at what a horrible thing we have done together."

We didn't want to shame our families, ourselves; His Dad a Pastor, mine a Deacon, ourselves Christians.

As we studied, we began to see the damage that abortion had done to us *both* and that hiding, and stuffing, and never talking about it was ***the*** major factor in our relationship difficulties. We had separated and almost divorced twenty plus years earlier. The abortion had come up in counseling, but no counselor ever tagged it as a problem or even something we needed to resolve.

As we continued in the *Surrendering the Secret* study, Steve shared that he had asked God's forgiveness for the abortion hundreds of times over the years. He had never asked mine. We have now forgiven *each other* for this grievous act and regretted mistake. We now live in the truth of God's forgiveness!

Steve said and I agree that the most meaningful part of the study, *if* we had to choose *one,* was the memorial time. The Peace of Release! Writing a letter to his child was difficult but freeing. Grief allowed. "Dear Son (we believe God revealed we had a son), I'm sorry <u>is not enough</u>! We snuffed you out before you had a chance. I'm sorry. I love you and long to see you." DAD!

I left planning the Memorial up to Steve. He said to bring the letters we'd written to our unborn child. Letters, books and Bible in tow, we got in the car. First stop was the grocery store. I was choosing a flower and here came Steve holding a balloon. I remember thinking that no one in the store had a clue why he was carrying this blue balloon. Not one but me. It felt like it was just God and us. Back in the car, I really had no idea where we were going, maybe a pretty hilltop or a park?

Steve turned into a beautiful cemetery. I gulped, but trusted.

Even though I walk through the valley of the shadow of death, I will fear no evil, for You are with me. Your rod and Your staff, they comfort me. (Psalm 23:4)

We read our letters and cried together, allowing ourselves, for the first time ever, to express our grief for this child. "This should've never happened. I miss him. I wish we'd known him." Steve released the balloon. Picked up by a wind, it headed straight for a group of trees. Clasping hands, we held our collective breath for a second as we watched that little blue circle bounce its way through a perfect archway of branches. We watched until it's Heavenward dance could no longer be seen. Closure. God is so good! We know that God has more for us, has healed us. Steve wrote in his book, and we both trust as stated in Joel 2:25, that God will continue to restore the years that were lost through shame and guilt and fear. We trust that God wants us to live for greater things than ourselves, to serve others and realize His power is revealed in our weakness!

I asked Steve, "Would you recommend that couples who've chosen abortion together do this study? YES! "Highly recommend?"

Tricia Heflin

Glenn and Jean

A "MAN'S" STORY ABOUT THE IMPACT OF ABORTION on His
Marriage

My name is Glenn and I am sixty-eight years old. I am a father
of an aborted child. It has taken forty-two years for me to be
able to share my story with anyone. This is my story.

On February 19, 1967, I married my high school and college
sweetheart. Jean graduated from college to be an elementary
school teacher. We were living in a small town in Mississippi
where Jean was teaching, and I was working for a metal
building manufacturer.

Life was good.

In the later part of that year, we found out that Jean had been
exposed to German measles. She was soon diagnosed with the
disease. Then we came to know that she was pregnant with
what would have been our first child. After the doctor
examined Jean and his explaining to us all the things that could
be wrong with our baby, he recommended that for Jean's
health, we should have a therapeutic abortion. What a
technical word to add to the front of the word abortion! In the
late 1960's abortions were not legal by law. The doctor said
nothing of the long-term side effects this action was going to
have on Jean and me.

We were both saved at an early age and were in church all
of our lives. For guidance in the decision, we called on our
pastor. Instead of his praying for healing, his advice was for us
to do what the doctor said and to have the abortion. We did
not find out until later that our pastor believed that life did not
begin until the baby breathed on its own.

Many years passed and I would not talk to Jean or friends about the abortion. I tried to block out of my mind, that when I signed that consent form, I gave the doctor permission to kill my baby. For years I would reason it out by what the doctor told me when he came out of the operating room. He said that Jean had already started dilating and that she would have probably had a miscarriage. Because of this I thought everything was ok.

I remember one morning Jean waking me up and telling me she had had a dream where she saw our baby wrapped in white in the arms of Jesus. She knew our baby was safe in heaven. Even with this thought in mind, I still did not want to talk to anyone about the abortion or admit that there was anything wrong with me.

When abortion became legal, more and more people talked openly about it. Every time I heard the word, all I could think about was, how this made Jean feel? All the time, it was eating me up inside. When I did speak to a friend about our first child, I would always say that we lost our first child by a therapeutic abortion—always putting emphasis on LOST and THERAPEUTIC.

Every year around the time of the abortion, Jean would start showing signs of depression. But I, being a workaholic, tried to never think about it. I thought, "I am a man. I can get through this all by myself!"

A couple of years ago Jean talked about going to a Sanctity of Human Life Service at our church. I remember telling her that if they start showing graphic pictures or describing what happens to a baby when aborted, I want you to get up and leave...you don't need that! Yet, through that special service, Jean signed up and went through a small group Bible study on

Abortion Recovery called, "Surrendering the Secret". The change in Jean's life was something to watch! She began to urge me to do a men's study on abortion recovery. I thought, "Who thinks about men needing this type of study?" It has come to my reality that men hurt also.

I went through a study and one particular scripture spoke to me. It is found in James 5:16: "Therefore confess your sins to one another and pray for one another, so that you may be healed." I found God's grace, mercy and forgiveness! I now know that my child is not lost but IS in the arms of our loving Lord and Savior, Jesus Christ. Through His strength I can live every day knowing He has forgiven me.

The scriptures tell us that He allows us to go through deep valleys and that He is with us and will strengthen us to go out on the other side. We are to use those experiences to help others. Jean and I are doing just that in speaking opportunities and leading small group studies, to teach others the effects of abortion in truth and love. Through the study of "Surrendering the Secret", my prayer is that whoever reads my story will come to know they too can have the peace that I have found. The secret lies in turning everything over to Jesus.

CONTACT surrenderingthesecret.com for information regarding couples' weekends and ministry.

Other Family Members Involved in Abortion

A Letter from a Grandfather

Dear Steven and Paul,

I have often thought of what it would have been like to have you as my grandsons while I am still living on this earth our God created for us. I was not fortunate enough to have a son of my own to do all the things guys enjoy doing together. We would have experienced many things together like snow and water skiing, golf, tennis, fishing, football and basketball. It would have been great fun to fly RC plans together. You would have taught me a few tricks I am sure.

You are grown young men now raised by our Heavenly Father. I am certain He has taken good care of you and these things we do in our brief time here on earth pale in comparison to our eternal experience.

Your mother was very young and afraid when you both came along. Although I cannot speak for her, I know she would have been a loving and caring mother. I take comfort in knowing the way of our Lord that you will welcome her with open arms when she comes to be with you in heaven. I believe her heart breaks for the loss of you not being with her here on earth.

Please ask our Lord to comfort her and give her peace.

With the love of your Grandfather and Grandmother and your Mother we will see you soon and forevermore.

Your Grandfather

CHAPTER THREE NOTES:

1 and 3: Medical and statistical information was taken from the article, "Medical Report/Women's Health/Abortion ... Is There a Connection?" NOEL: noelinfo@noelforlife.org, accessed October 25, 2006.

2: "Abortion Data" from Reports of the Alan Guttmacher Institute: www.religioustolerance.org/abo_fact3.htm, accessed November 15, 2006.

CLOSING WORDS

Think back to the first time you opened this book. You were in one of two places; you were either someone who has endured the heartbreak of a past abortion or you were someone who simply cares about those who have. Either way, now that you have completed A Surrendered Life, my prayer is that you are equipped in a whole new way.

You are SET FREE by threads of forgiveness, hope and grace.

Your inspiration to confront and join God's voice for life has climbed to a whole new level of strength and courage. Your identity is no longer that of a post-abortive woman or man. You are a child of God, of truth and integrity. Your identity is in Christ and who He says you are. You are a new creation in Christ. God has been faithful to do what He said He would do. He has set YOU FREE!

Although you have completed A Surrendered Life, the rest of your life is a continuing journey with Christ. There will always be mountains to climb until we reach our Heavenly destination.

Thank you for joining me on THIS journey. As we part, I hope to hear from you, possibly by email or maybe even a good old-fashioned letter.

ABOUT THE AUTHOR

Pat's most precious role is being "Honey" (aka WIFE of forty plus years) to Mike, mom to three amazing adults, mother-in-law to two beautiful women and "G" to five PERFECT grandchildren. Pat is a busy national speaker and author. She writes articles for newspapers, blogs, newsletters, and ministry media, including Lifeway, Focus on the Family and Proverbs 31 Ministries.

Pat is Founder of a pregnancy resource center based in Tampa, Florida that has become one of the nation's largest sanctity of life ministries. Pat's healing program for *Surrendering the Secret*, was published by LifeWay Christian Resources in 2009 and updated in 2019 and includes a leader's guide and DVD series. The ministry headquarters are located in Atlanta, Georgia. Through her National leadership staff and over 3,000 International partners and churches, the ministry provides ministry support groups to men, women and couples' all over the world.

Pat shares her daily life both the messes and the ministry, through her website and blog at www.patlayton.net.

Surrendering the

HEART

—— *of a* ——

FATHER

A Man's Guide
to Abortion Recovery

PAT AND MIKE LAYTON

Help *Heal* The Heartbreak of Abortion
in Your Church and Community!

Sources believe as many as 40% of women of childbearing
age have experienced a past abortion.

Women are hurting everywhere, often **silently.**

Will *YOU* lead the way?

Help give a *priceless* gift of healing to a woman
Share in her JOY when she experiences *freedom*
Create a lasting friendship
Share TRUTH

Say *YES* and make a difference!

If you are interested in providing STS through your church,
counseling organization or pregnancy resource center please
check out our website at www.surrenderingthesecret.com

PAT LAYTON

Visit Patlayton.net

Please join Pat in the social media playground today for up-to-date happenings, including more information about speaking engagements, events, free gifts, products and MORE!

 http://patlayton.net

 https://www.facebook.com/patlayton.author

https://www.instagram.com/patlayton

https://twitter.com/patricialayton

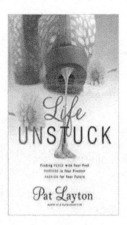

Join other women as we work our way from dizzy, desperate, and digging to a

Life Unstuck!

www.life-unstuck.com / www.patlayton.net

Made in United States
Orlando, FL
01 June 2022

18374912R00108